THE Lyric LIBRARY

Christmas

Complete Lyrics for 200 Songs

P9-AON-271

HAL•LEONARD®

Other books in *The Lyric Library*:

Broadway Volume I
Broadway Volume II
Classic Rock
Contemporary Christian
Country
Early Rock 'n' Roll
Love Songs
Pop/Rock Ballads

ISBN 0-634-04547-4

Library of Congress cataloguing-in-publication data has been applied for.

Visit Hal Leonard Online at
www.halleonard.com

Preface

Songs have an uncanny ability to burrow deep into our gray matter, sometimes lying dormant for years or decades before something pings them back into our consciousness. All kinds of songs reside in there, more than we can count—not just songs we love and intentionally memorized and have sung again and again, but songs we once heard in passing, songs that form a soundtrack to significant people and places and moments in our lives, and even (or especially) songs that drive us crazy, like the chirping TV jingle that still won't let go years after the product it plugged has disappeared from the shelves.

Most of the time, though, our memories of songs are frustratingly incomplete unless we actively maintain them. The first verse and chorus that we blare out in the shower or at the holiday party degenerates into mumbled lines, disconnected phrases, and bits and pieces inadvertently lifted from other songs. And, of course, there's the likelihood that what we *do* remember is riddled with mondegreens, or misheard lyrics. In these pages you'll find many opportunities to bring a little more completeness and accuracy to your Christmas repertoire (how about the second and third verses of "Jingle Bells"?), as well as to rediscover a nearly forgotten gem, wallow in nostalgia, or just browse through some enduring examples of the songwriter's craft.

In contemporary American life, no body of music can quite compete with the depth, variety, and longevity of Christmas songs—they're the closest thing we have to a universal repertoire, known and sung way beyond the Christian devout and surrounding us from the moment the Thanksgiving turkey is stowed away in the fridge (or even earlier) up through the last clinking glass and chorus of "Auld Lang Syne" on New Year's Eve. These songs' origins span hundreds of years and just about every genre you can think of—classical, gospel, jazz, rock, blues, country, folk traditions from around the globe.... Many of the themes are sacred, of course, or celebrate hearth and home and the icy beauty of winter, but there's also the tongue-in-cheek counterpoint of songs like "Grandma's Killer Fruitcake"—satirical and novelty Christmas songs are a genre unto themselves. Whatever their angle or style, songwriters just can't seem to resist contributing to the Christmas repertoire, and we can't resist revisiting it year after year.

Contents

Christmas

A Caroling We Go

Music and Lyrics by Johnny Marks

A caroling, a caroling, a caroling we go,
Hearts filled with music and cheeks aglow.
From house to house we bring the message of the King again,
Peace on Earth, goodwill to men,
Peace on Earth, goodwill to men.

We bring you season's greetings and we wish the best to you,
And may our wish last the whole year through.
Come join us if you will as we are singing once again,
Peace on Earth, goodwill to men,
Peace on Earth, goodwill to men.

Now you may have your holly and perhaps some mistletoe,
Maybe a fir tree and maybe snow.
But wouldn't it be wonderful if we could have again,
Peace on Earth, goodwill to men,
Peace on Earth, goodwill to men.

Repeat Verse 1

All My Heart This Night Rejoices

Words and Music by Johann Ebeling and Catherine Winkworth

All my heart this night rejoices,
As I hear, far and near,
Sweetest angel voices.
"Christ is born," their choirs are singing,
Till the air ev'rywhere
Now with joy is ringing.

Hark, a voice from yonder manger,
Soft and sweet, doth entreat,
"Flee from woe and danger.
Brethren, come from all grieves you.
You are freed; all you need
I will surely give you."

Come then, let us hasten yonder.
Here let all, great and small,
Kneel in awe and wonder.
Love Him who with love is yearning.
Hail the star that from far
Bright with hope is burning.

All Through the Night

Welsh Folksong

Sleep, my Child, and peace attend Thee,
All through the night;
Guardian angels God will send thee,
All through the night.
Soft the drowsy hours are creeping,
Hill and vale in slumber sleeping,
God His loving vigil keeping,
All through the night.

While the moon her watch is keeping,
All through the night;
While the weary world is sleeping,
All through the night,
Through your dreams you're softly stealing,
Visions of delight revealing,
Christmas time is so appealing,
All through the night.

You, my God, a Babe of wonder,
All through the night;
Dreams you dream can't break from thunder,
All through the night.
Children's dreams cannot be broken;
Life is but a lovely token.
Christmas should be softly spoken
All through the night.

Almost Day

Words and Music by Huddie Ledbetter

Chickens a-crowin' for midnight, it's almost day;
Chickens a-crowin' for midnight, it's almost day.
Candy canes and sugar plums, on Christmas Day;
Candy canes and sugar plums, on Christmas Day.

Mama'll stuff a turkey on Christmas Day;
Mama'll stuff a turkey on Christmas Day.
Santa Claus is coming on Christmas Day;
Santa Claus is coming on Christmas Day.

Angels from the Realms of Glory

Words by James Montgomery
Music by Henry T. Smart

Angels from the realms of glory,
Wing your flight o'er all the earth;
Ye who sang creation's story,
Now proclaim Messiah's birth.

Refrain:
Come and worship!
Come and worship!
Worship Christ the newborn King!

Shepherds in the fields abiding,
Watching o'er your flocks by night,
God with man is now residing;
Yonder shines the infant Light.

Refrain

Sages, leave your contemplations,
Brighter visions beam afar,
Seek the great Desire of nations,
Ye have seen His natal star.

Refrain

Saints before the altar bending,
Watching long in hope and fear,
Suddenly the Lord, descending,
In His temple shall appear

Refrain

Angels We Have Heard on High

Traditional French Carol
Translated by James Chadwick

Angels we have heard on high,
Singing sweetly o'er the plains,
And the mountains in reply
Echoing their joyous strains.

Refrain:
Gloria in excelsis Deo,
Gloria in excelsis Deo.

Shepherds, why this jubilee?
Why your joyous strains prolong?
What the gladsome tidings be
Which inspire your heavenly song?

Refrain

Come to Bethlehem and see
Him whose birth the angels sing.
Come adore on bended knee
Christ the Lord, the newborn King.

Refrain

See within a manger laid
Jesus, Lord of heav'n and earth!
Mary, Joseph, lend your aid;
With us sing our Savior's birth.

Refrain

As Lately We Watched

19th Century Austrian Carol

As lately we watched
O'er our fields through the night,
A star there was seen
Of such glorious light!
All through the night,
Angels did sing
In carols so sweet
Of the birth of a King.

A King of such beauty
Was ne'er before seen,
And Mary, His mother,
So like to a queen.
Blest be the hour,
Welcome the morn,
For Christ, our dear Savior,
On earth now is born.

Then shepherds, be joyful,
Salute your liege King;
Let hills and dales ring
To the song that ye sing:
Blest be the hour,
Welcome the morn,
For Christ, our dear Savior,
On earth now is born.

As with Gladness Men of Old

Words by William Chatterton Dix
Music by Conrad Kocher

As with gladness men of old
Did the guiding star behold;
As with joy they hailed its light,
Leading onward, beaming bright;
So, most gracious Lord, may we
Evermore be led to Thee.

As with joyful steps they sped
To that lowly manger bed,
There to bend the knee before
Him whom heav'n and earth adore;
So may we with willing feet
Ever seek thy mercy seat.

As they offered gifts most rare
At that manger rude and bare;
So may we with holy joy,
Pure and free from sin's alloy,
All our costliest treasures bring,
Christ, to Thee, our heav'nly King.

Holy Jesus, ev'ry day
Keep us in the narrow way;
And when earthly things are past,
Bring our ransomed souls at last
Where they need no star to guide,
Where no clouds Thy glory hide.

As Long as There's Christmas

Music by Rachel Portman
Lyrics by Don Black

from the film Walt Disney's *Beauty and the Beast–The Enchanted Christmas*

Female:
There is more to this time of year
Than sleighbells and holly,

Male:
Misteltoe and snow.

Both:
Those things will come and go.

Female:
Don't look inside a stocking.
Don't look under the tree.
The one thing we're looking for
Is something we can't see.

Male:
Far more precious than silver
And more splendid than gold,
This is something to treasure,
But it's something we can't hold.

Both:
As long as there's Christmas, I truly believe

Male:
That hope is the greatest

Both:
Of the gifts we'll receive,

Male:
We'll receive.
As we all pray together, it's a time to rejoice.

Female:
And though we may look diff'rent,

Both:
We'll all sing with one voice.

Male:
Whoa.

Both:
As long as there's Christmas, I truly believe
That hope is the greatest of the
   gifts we'll receive.
As long as there's Christmas,
   we'll all be just fine.
A star shines above us,

Female:
Lighting your way

Male:
And mine.

Female:
Oh.

Male:
Light my way.

THE LYRIC LIBRARY

Female:
You know I will.

Both:
As long as there's Christmas, I truly believe
That hope is the greatest of the
    gifts we'll receive.
As long as our guiding star shines above,
There'll always be Christmas,

Male:
So there always will be a time

Both:
When the world is filled with peace and love.

Auld Lang Syne

Words by Robert Burns
Traditional Scottish Melody

Should auld acquaintance be forgot,
And never brought to mind?
Should auld acquaintance be forgot
And days of Auld Lang Syne?

For Auld Lang Syne, my dear,
For Auld Lang Syne,
We'll take a cup of kindness yet
For Auld Lang Syne.

Away in a Manger

Traditional
Words by John T. McFarland (v.3)
Music by James R. Murray

Away in a manger, no crib for His bed,
The little Lord Jesus lay down His sweet head;
The stars in the bright sky looked down where he lay,
The little Lord Jesus, asleep in the hay.

The cattle are lowing, the baby awakes,
But little Lord Jesus no crying he makes.
I love Thee, Lord Jesus! Look down from the sky,
And stay by my side until morning is nigh.

Be near me, Lord Jesus; I ask Thee to stay
Close by me forever, and love me, I pray.
Bless all the dear children in Thy tender care,
And take us to heaven, to live with Thee there.

Baby, It's Cold Outside

By Frank Loesser

from the Motion Picture *Neptune's Daughter*
a standard recorded by various artists

*Note: The song is a duet; the male lines
    are in parentheses.*

I really can't stay,
(But baby it's cold outside!)
I've got to go 'way.
(But baby it's cold outside!)
This evening has been
(Been hoping that you'd drop in!)
So very nice.
(I'll hold your hands they're just like ice.)
My mother will start to worry
(Beautiful, what's your hurry?)
And father will be pacing the floor.
(Listen to the fireplace roar!)
So really I'd better scurry,
(Beautiful, please don't hurry.)
Well, maybe just half a drink more.
(Put some records on while I pour.)
The neighbors might think
(But, baby it's bad out there.)
Say, what's in the drink?
(No cabs to be had out there.)
I wish I knew how
(Your eyes are like starlight now)
To break the spell.
(I'll take your hat your hair looks swell.)
I ought to say "No, no, no, Sir!"
(Mind if I move in closer?)
At least I'm gonna say that I tried.
(What's the sense of hurting my pride.)
I really can't stay
(Oh, baby, don't hold out,)
Ah, but it's cold outside.
(Baby, it's cold outside.)

I simply must go.
(But baby it's cold outside!)
The answer is no!
(But baby it's cold outside!)
The welcome has been,
(How lucky that you dropped in!)
So nice and warm.
(Look out the window at that storm.)
My sister will be suspicious,
(Gosh, your lips look delicious.)
My brother will be there at the door.
(Waves upon a tropical shore!)
My maiden aunt's mind is vicious.
(Gosh, your lips are delicious)
Well, maybe just a cigarette more.
(Never such a blizzard before.)
I've got to get home
(But, baby, you'd freeze out there)
Say, lend me a comb.
(It's up to your knees out there.)

You've really been grand,
(I thrill when you touch my hand)
But don't you see.
(How can you do this thing to me.)
There's bound to be talk tomorrow.
(Think of my life-long sorrow.)
At least there will be plenty implied.
(If you caught pneumonia and died.)
I really can't stay
(Get over that old doubt,)
Ah, but it's cold outside.
(Baby, it's cold outside.)

© 1948 (Renewed) FRANK MUSIC CORP.

Because It's Christmas (For All the Children)

Music by Barry Manilow
Lyric by Bruce Sussman and Jack Feldman

Tonight the stars shine for the children.
And light the way for dreams to fly.
Tonight our love comes wrapped in ribbons.
The world is right and hopes are high.
And from a dark and frosted window
A child appears to search the sky
Because it's Christmas, because it's Christmas.

Tonight belongs to all the children.
Tonight the joy rings through the air.
And so, we send our tender blessings
To all the children ev'rywhere,
To see the smiles and hear the laughter;
A time to give, a time to share,
Because it's Christmas for now and forever
For all the children and for the children in us all.

Repeat Verse 2

Bethlehem Morning

Words and Music by Morris Chapman

Lift up your heads, no need to mourn,
His hand is stretched out still.
For unto us a Child is born,
His promise to fulfill.
Jerusalem, He cried for you,
He did not come to you in vain.
His loving arms are open wide for you,
And He will come, He will come again.

Bethlehem morning
Is more than just a memory,
For the child that was born there
Has come to set us free.
Bethlehem sunrise,
I can see Him in your eyes,
For the Child that was born there,
His Spirit never dies.
His star will never,
Will never grow dim,
And it's a brand new dawn,
A new Jerusalem,
And we, and we will reign,
We will reign with Him.

Bethlehem morning
Is more than just a memory,
For the child that was born there
Has come to set us free.
Bethlehem sunrise,
I can see Him in your eyes,
For the Child that was born there,
He is the King of Kings,
And the Lord of Lords,
And He will come again.

The Birthday of a King

Words and Music by William H. Neidlinger

In the little village of Bethlehem,
There lay a Child one day.
And the sky was bright with a holy light
O'er the place where Jesus lay.

Refrain:
Alleluia, o how the angels sang!
Alleluia, how it rang!
And the sky was bright with a holy light;
'Twas the birthday of a King!

'Twas a humble birthplace, but oh, how much
God gave to us that day!
From the manger bed what a path has led,
What a perfect holy way.

Refrain

The Boar's Head Carol

Traditional English

The boar's head in hand bear I,
Bedecked with bays and rosemary.
And I pray you, my masters, merry be,
Quot estes in convivio.
Caput apri defero,
Redens laudes Domino.

The boar's head, I understand,
The finest dish in all the land,
Which is thus all bedecked with gay garland,
Let us servire cantico.
Caput apri defero,
Redens laudes Domino.

Our steward hath provided this,
In honor of the King of bliss,
Which on this day to be served is,
In Reginensi atrio.
Caput apri defero,
Redens laudes Domino.

Breath of Heaven (Mary's Song)

Words and Music by Amy Grant and Chris Eaton

I have traveled many moonless nights,
Cold and weary, with a babe inside.
And I wonder what I've done.
Holy Father, you have come
And chosen me now, to carry your son.

I am waiting in a silent prayer.
I am frightened by the load I bear.
In a world as cold as stone,
Must I walk this path alone?

Be with me now,
Be with me now.

Refrain:
Breath of heaven, hold me together.
Be forever near me, breath of heaven.
Breath of heaven, lighten my darkness,
Pour over me your holiness,
For you are holy, breath of heaven.

Do you wonder, as you watch my face,
If a wiser one should have had my place?
But I offer all I am
For the mercy of your plan.
Help me be strong, help me be, help me.

Refrain

Bring a Torch, Jeannette, Isabella

17th Century French Provençal Carol

Bring a torch, Jeannette, Isabella,
Bring a torch, come swiftly and run.
Christ is born, tell the folk of the village,
Jesus is sleeping in His cradle,
Ah, ah, beautiful is the Mother,
Ah, ah, beautiful is her Son.

Hasten now, good folk of the village,
Hasten now, the Christ Child to see.
You will find him asleep in a manger,
Quietly come and whisper softly,
Hush, hush, peacefully now He slumbers,
Hush, hush, peacefully now He sleeps.

Burgundian Carol

Words and Music by Oscar Brand

The winter season of the year,
When to the world our Lord was born,
The ox and donkey, so they say,
Did keep His Holy Presence warm.
How many oxen and donkeys now,
If they were there when first He came,
How many oxen and donkeys you know
At such a time would do the same?

As soon as to these humble beasts
Appeared our Lord, so mild and sweet,
With joy they knelt before His grace,
And gently kissed His tiny feet.
If we, like oxen and donkeys then,
In spite of all the things we've heard,
Would be like oxen and donkeys then,
We'd hear the truth, believe His word.

C-H-R-I-S-T-M-A-S

Words by Jenny Lou Carson
Music by Eddy Arnold

When I was but a youngster Christmas meant one thing:
That I'd be getting lots of toys that day.
I learned a whole lot diff'rent when mother sat me down
And taught me to spell Christmas this way.

C is for the Christ child born upon this day,
H for herald angels in the night.
R means our Redeemer,
I means Israel,
S is for the star that shone so bright.
T is for three wise men, they who traveled far,
M is for the manger where He lay.
A's for all He stands for,
S means shepherds came,
And that's why there's a Christmas day.

Carol of the Birds

Traditional Catalonian Carol

Upon this wond'rous night,
When God's great star appears,
And floods the earth with brightness,
Birds' voices rise in song,
And, warbling all night long,
Express their glad hearts' lightness.
Birds' voices rise in song,
And, warbling all night long,
Express their glad hearts' lightness.

The Nightingale is first
To bring his song of praise,
And tell us of his gladness:
"Jesus, our Lord, is born
To free us from all sin,
And banish ev'ry sadness!
Jesus, our Lord, is born
To free us from all sin
And banish ev'ry sadness!"

The answ'ring Sparrow cries:
"God comes to earth this day
Amid the angels soaring."
Trilling in sweetest tones,
The Finch his Lord now owns:
"To Him be all thanksgiving."
Trilling in sweetest tones,
The Finch his Lord now owns:
"To Him be all thanksgiving."

The Partridge adds these words:
"To Bethlehem I'll fly,
Where in the stall He's lying.
There, near the manger blest,
I'll build myself a nest,
And sing my love undying.
There, near the manger blest,
I'll build myself a nest,
And sing my love undying."

Caroling, Caroling

Words by Wihla Hutson
Music by Alfred Burt

Caroling, caroling, now we go,
Christmas bells are ringing!
Caroling, caroling through the snow,
Christmas bells are ringing!
Joyous voices sweet and clear,
Sing the sad of heart to cheer.
Ding, dong, ding, dong,
Christmas bells are ringing!

Caroling, caroling through the town,
Christmas bells are ringing!
Caroling, caroling up and down,
Christmas bells are ringing!
Mark ye well the song we sing,
Gladsome tidings now we bring.
Ding, dong, ding, dong,
Christmas bells are ringing!

Caroling, caroling, near and far,
Christmas bells are ringing!
Following, following yonder star,
Christmas bells are ringing!
Sing we all this happy morn,
"Lo, the King of heav'n is born!"
Ding, dong, ding, dong,
Christmas bells are ringing!

Child of Bethlehem

Words by Wayne Watson and Claire Cloninger
Music by Wayne Watson

Still, quiet night in Bethlehem;
Earth's sleeps and few take thought of Him.
But the heavens rejoice! And the angels sing!
The Child of Bethlehem is the King of kings!

Still, wise men worship at His feet,
And lost souls awaken from their sleep.
And the heav'ns rejoice! And the angels sing!
The Child of Bethlehem is the King of kings!

Down from heaven's glory, to a manger bed;
Crucified, glorified: He was born to be our Savoir!

Come, children over all the earth.
Come and celebrate the Savior's birth!
Ev'ry knee shall bow and ev'ry nation sing!
The Child of Bethlehem is the King of kings!

Come, children over all the earth.
Come, and celebrate the Savior's birth!
Ev'ry knee shall bow and ev'ry nation sing!
The Child of Bethlehem, He is the King of kings!
The Child of Bethlehem is the King of kings!

Child of Peace

Words and Music by Bob Farrell

On a night of promise long ago
When a star announced the light of hope
To a world that knew no peace before,
The holy Child of peace was born.
But He stirred their longings deep within
For His kingdom knew no end.
From a place eternal, high above,
The wondrous Child of peace had come.

Child of comfort, Child of light;
Hope that drives away the night.
Touch our lives from heaven above
Oh, Child of peace, we need Your love.

In a world where peace eludes us still,
Where the heart exerts its will;
At a time when words are not enough,
Oh, Child of peace, we need Your love.
Oh, Man of peace, we need Your love.
God who only knows our need,
Come to us, o Child of peace.

The Chipmunk Song

Words and Music by Ross Bagdasarian

Christmas, Christmas time is near,
Time for toys and time for cheer.
We've been good but we can't last,
Hurry Christmas, hurry fast!
Want a plane that loops the loop;
Me, I want a hula hoop.
We can hardly stand the wait,
Please, Christmas, don't be late.

Christians, Awake! Salute the Happy Morn

Traditional

Christians, awake, salute the happy morn
Whereon the Savior of mankind was born;
Rise to adore the mystery of love
Which hosts of angels chanted from above;
With them the joyful tidings first begun
Of God incarnate and the Virgin's Son.

Then to the watchful shepherds it was told,
Who heard th'angelic herald's voice: "Behold,
I bring good tidings of a Savior's birth
To you and all the nations upon earth;
This day hath God fulfilled His promised word;
This day is born a Savior, Christ the Lord."

He spake; and straightway the celestial choir
In hymns of joy, unknown before, conspire;
The praises of redeeming love they sang
And heav'n's whole orb with alleluias rang;
God's highest glory was their anthem still,
Peace on the earth, and unto men good will.

Then may we hope, th'angelic hosts among,
To sing, redeemed, a glad triumphal song;
He that was born upon this joyful day
Around us all His glory shall display;
Saved by His love, incessant we shall sing
Eternal praise to heaven's almighty King.

Christmas Is a Homemade Holiday

By Annie Dinerman and Ned Ginsburg

Each Christmas as you think
About the things you're grateful for,
You bow your head and pray
That the tree will fit through the door.
A snowman cookie makes the job
A lot more fun to do.
You smile because it's awf'lly rich, mm,
And just for a moment, so are you.

Christmas is a homemade holiday; fix it family style.
Season with this sweetest memories, mix it a while.
Stir in hugs and kisses; you'll get lots of those,
With mistletoe above you and flour upon your nose.
Christmas is a time for sprinkling spice and sparkle and joy;
Simmer 'til it's warm and sincere.
It's a yearly miracle that ev'ryone understands,
For it's made with love and your own two hands.

Christmas is a homemade holiday, one you'll never outgrow.
Funny how a pile of cottonballs turns into snow.
Kids in tinsel halos give a manger play,
And Mom believes her rascals are angels for a day.
Christmas is the time for twinkling lights and startling sights;
Driveways glow with wise men and deer.
It's a yearly miracle that ev'ryone understands,
For it's made with love and your own two hands.

Christmas Is A-Coming (May God Bless You)

Words and Music by Frank Luther

When I'm feelin' blue, an' when I'm feelin' low,
Then I start to think about the happiest man I know;
He doesn't mind the snow an' he doesn't mind the rain,
But all December you will hear him at your windowpane,
A-singin' again an' again an' again an' again an' again.

Christmas is a-comin' and the geese are getting' fat,
Please to put a penny in a poor man's hat.
If you haven't got a penny, a ha' penny'll do,
If you haven't got a ha' penny, may God bless you.
God bless you, gentlemen, God bless you,
If you haven't got a ha' penny, may God bless you.

Christmas is a-comin' and the lights are on the tree,
How about a turkey leg for poor old me?
If you haven't got a turkey leg, a turkey wing'll do,
If you haven't got a turkey wing, may God bless you.
God bless you, gentlemen, God bless you,
If you haven't got a turkey wing, may God bless you.

Christmas is a-comin' and the egg is in the nog,
Please to let me sit around your old yule log.
If you'd rather I didn't sit around, to stand around'll do,
If you'd rather I didn't stand around, may God bless you.
God bless you, gentlemen, God bless you,
If you'd rather I didn't stand around, may God bless you.
If you haven't got a thing for me, may God bless you.

Christmas Is Just About Here

Words and Music by Loonis McGlohon

It's fun hanging 'round in the kitchen,
Where ev'rything smells so nice;
Oh, Mama is a baking a fruitcake
With apples, honey, and spice.
The children are getting excited
Whenever gray clouds appear;
The almanac promised a snowfall,
And Christmas is just about here.

'Tis the season to be jolly,
Ev'rybody feels young.
Deck the halls with boughs of holly
And let the stockings be hung.
We'll soon have a visit from Saint Nick,
And maybe he'll bring reindeer.
We never outgrow the warm feeling
When Christmas is just about here.

Ev'rybody has a list of things to do.
Buy a tie for Dad which will look good
    with blue.
Did you mail Aunt Mary a Christmas card?
Tie a ribbon on the lamppost out
    in the yard.

It's great fun when Papa will take us
To pick out a Christmas tree;
Mom says to be sure that we choose one
That's big and taller than me.
It's time to start wrapping the presents
For ev'ryone we hold dear,
Then hiding them back in the closet,
'Cause Christmas is just about here.

Deck the halls with boughs of holly,
Fill up the candy jar.
Light a candle in the window
And hang up the Christmas star.
I like ev'rything about Christmas,
The holly and holiday cheer.
Let's hurry up and get ready,
'Cause Christmas is just about here.

TRO - © Copyright 1984 and 1985 Melody Trails, Inc., New York, NY

The Christmas Shoes

Words and Music by Leonard Ahlstrom and Eddie Carswell

It was almost Christmas time;
There I stood in another line,
Tryin' to buy that last gift or two,
Not really in the Christmas mood.
Standin' right in front of me
Was a little boy waiting anxiously,
Pacin' 'round like little boys do,
And in his hands he held a pair of shoes.
And his clothes were worn and old,
He was dirty from head to toe.
But when it came his time to pay,
I couldn't believe what I heard him say.

Refrain:
"Sir, I wanna buy these shoes for
    my mama, please.
It's Christmas Eve and these shoes
    are just her size.
Could you hurry, sir? Daddy says
    there's not much time.
You see, she's been sick for quite a while
And I know these shoes will make
    her smile,
And I want her to look beautiful if Mama
    meets Jesus tonight."

They counted pennies for what
    seemed like years,
Then the cashier said,
    "Son, there's not enough here."
He searched his pockets frantic'lly,
Then he turned and he looked at me.
He said, "Mama always made Christmas
    good at our house,
Though most years she just did without.
Tell me, sir, what am I gonna do?
Somehow, I've gotta buy these
    Christmas shoes."
So I laid the money down.
I just had to help him out.
And I'll never forget the look on his face
When he said, "Mama's gonna
    look so great."

Refrain

I knew I'd caught a glimpse of heaven's love
As he thanked me and ran out.
I knew that God had sent that little boy
To remind me just what Christmas
    is all about.

Refrain

The Christmas Song
(Chestnuts Roasting on an Open Fire)

Music and Lyric by Mel Torme and Robert Wells

Chestnuts roasting on an open fire,
Jack Frost nipping at your nose,
Yuletide carols being sung by a choir,
And folks dressed up like Eskimos.

Ev'rybody knows a turkey and some mistletoe
Help to make the season bright.
Tiny tots with their eyes all aglow
Will find it hard to sleep tonight.

They know that Santa's on his way;
He's loaded lots of toys and goodies on his sleigh,
And every mother's child is gonna spy
To see if reindeer really know how to fly.

And so I'm offering this simple phrase
To kids from one to ninety-two.
Although it's been said many times, many ways,
"Merry Christmas to you."

Christmas Time Is Here

Words by Lee Mendelson
Music by Vince Guaraldi

from the television special *A Charlie Brown Christmas*

Christmas time is here,
Happiness and cheer.
Fun for all that children call
Their fav'rite time of year.

Snowflakes in the air,
Carols ev'rywhere.
Olden times and ancient rhymes
Of love and dreams to share.

Refrain:
Sleigh bells in the air,
Beauty ev'rywhere.
Yuletide by the fireside
And joyful mem'ries there.
Christmas time is here,
We'll be drawing near.
Oh, that we could always see
Such spirit through the year.

Repeat Refrain

The Christmas Waltz

Words by Sammy Cahn
Music by Jule Styne

Frosted window panes,
Candles gleaming inside,
Painted candy canes on the tree;
Santa's on his way,
He's filled his sleigh with things,
Things for you and for me.

It's the time of year
When the world falls in love,
Ev'ry song you hear seems to say:
"Merry Christmas,
May your New Year dreams come true."
And this song of mine,
In three-quarter time,
Wishes you and yours
The same thing too.

Come, Thou Long-Expected Jesus

Words by Charles Wesley
Music adapted by Henry J. Gauntlett

Come, Thou long-expected Jesus,
Born to set Thy people free.
From our fears and sins release us;
Let us find our rest in Thee.
Israel's strength and consolation,
Hope of all the earth Thou art;
Dear desire of ev'ry nation,
Joy of ev'ry longing heart.

Born Thy people to deliver,
Born a child and yet a king,
Born to reign in us forever,
Now Thy gracious kingdom bring.
By Thine own eternal Spirit
Rule in all our hearts alone.
By Thine all sufficient merit,
Raise us to Thy glorious throne.

The Coventry Carol

Traditional

Lullay, thou little tiny child,
By by, lully lullay.
Lullay, thou little tiny child,
By by, lully lullay.

O sisters too, how may we do,
For to preserve this day.
This poor youngling for whom we sing,
By by, lully lullay.

Herod the king, in his raging,
Charged he hath this day.
His men of might, in his own sight,
All young children to slay.

That woe is me, poor child for thee!
And ever morn and day,
For thy parting nor say nor sing,
By by, lully lullay.

A Cradle in Bethlehem

Words and Music by Al Bryan and Lawrence Stock

Refrain:
Sing sweet and low your lullaby
Till angels say, "Amen."
A mother tonight is rocking
A cradle in Bethlehem.

While wise men follow through the dark
A star that beckons them,
A mother tonight is rocking
A cradle in Bethlehem.

"A little Child shall lead them,"
The prophets said of old.
In storm and tempest heed them
Until the bell is tolled.

Refrain Twice

Deck the Hall

Traditional Welsh Carol

Deck the hall with boughs of holly,
Fa la la la la, la la la la.
'Tis the season to be jolly,
Fa la la la la, la la la la.
Don we now our gay apparel,
Fa la la, la la la, la la la.
Troll the ancient Yuletide carol,
Fa la la la la, la la la la.

See the blazing yule before us,
Fa la la la la, la la la la.
Strike the harp and join the chorus,
Fa la la la la, la la la la.
Follow me in merry measure,
Fa la la, la la la, la la la.
While I tell of Yuletide treasure,
Fa la la la la, la la la la.

Fast away the old year passes,
Fa la la la la, la la la la.
Hail the new, ye lads and lasses,
Fa la la la la, la la la la.
Sing we joyous, all together,
Fa la la, la la la, la la la.
Heedless of the wind and weather,
Fa la la la la, la la la la.

Ding Dong! Merrily on High

French Carol

Ding dong! Merrily on high,
In heav'n the bells are ringing.
Ding dong! Verily the sky
Is riv'n with angel singing.

Refrain:
Gloria, Hosanna in excelsis!

E'en so here below, below,
Let steeple bells be swungen,
And io, io, io,
By priest and people sungen.

Refrain

Do They Know It's Christmas?

Words and Music by M. Ure and B. Geldof

It's Christmastime, there's no need to be afraid.
At Christmastime, we let in light and we banish shade.
And in our world of plenty we can spread a smile of joy.
Throw your arms around the world at Christmastime,
But say a prayer, to pray for the other ones at Christmastime.

It's hard, but when you're having fun,
There's a world outside your window.
And it's a world of dread and fear
Where the only water flowing is the bitter sting of tears.
And the Christmas bells that ring there
Are the clanging chimes of doom.
Well, tonight, thank God it's them instead of you.
And there won't be snow in Africa this Christmastime,
The greatest gift they'll get this year is life.
Oh, where nothing ever grows, no rain or rivers flow,
Do they know it's Christmastime at all?

Here's to you, raise a glass for ev'ryone;
Here's to them, underneath that burning sun.
Do they know it's Christmastime at all?

Feed the world.
Feed the world.
Feed the world.
Let them know it's Christmastime again.
Let them know it's Christmastime again.

Do You Hear What I Hear

Words and Music by Noel Regney and Gloria Shayne

Said the night wind to the little lamb,
"Do you see what I see?
Way up in the sky, little lamb,
Do you see what I see?
A star, a star, dancing in the night,
With a tail as big as a kite,
With a tail as big as a kite."

Said the little lamb to the shepherd boy,
"Do you hear what I hear?
Ringing through the sky, shepherd boy,
Do you hear what I hear?
A song, a song, high above the tree,
With a voice as big as the sea,
With a voice as big as the sea."

Said the shepherd boy to the mighty king,
"Do you know what I know?
In your palace warm, mighty king,
Do you know what I know?
A Child, a Child shivers in the cold;
Let us bring Him silver and gold,
Let us bring Him silver and gold."

Said the king to the people ev'rywhere,
"Listen to what I say!
Pray for peace, people ev'rywhere,
Listen to what I say!
The Child, the Child, sleeping in the night,
He will bring us goodness and light,
He will bring us goodness and light."

Don't Make Me Play That Grandma Song Again

Words and Music by Elmo Shropshire and Rita Abrams

Spoken:
Allow me to introduce myself,
I'm Elwood the midnight D.J.
On radio station KHICK.
Now I try to run a quality show
And all my fans will tell you so,
Except at Christmas much to my dismay.

Refrain:
Oh no, don't make me play
That grandma song again!
Though that request line glows and glows,
Just as bright as Rudolph's nose.
I'll do anything you say,
I'll play those barkin' dogs all day,
But please don't make me play
That grandma song again!

Spoken:
And now a word from our sponsor.

Now ev'ry Christmas I get frosted,
When poor Grandma got accosted,
And all them weirdos enjoy her suffering.
And that Elmo guy just keeps on smilin'
While them royalties keep on pilin',
And the worst part is
He can't even sing!

Refrain

Spoken:
Friends! It's that time of year again
That makes you just wanna get out there
    and charge!
And while you're doin' it,
Why not have, playin' in the background,
Our collector's set of twenty-four
Of the most beloved Christmas carols
    of all time.
Classics like "You Bumped Your
    Noggin on my Tobbogan"
Or "Hey! Hey! Grampa's Got a
    Brand New Nag"!
To order now dial one nine hundred
    fruitcake.
And now back to you, Elwood.

Thanks, Elmer, so anywho,
I told the station manager
He'd have to choose between me and her,
Because that grandma song is a moral
    abomination!
So, he says, "Son, our ratings are fine.
And furthermore, our sponsors are buyin',
And I'm transferrin' you to the
    FM classical station!"

Refrain, Ending with:
But please don't make me play that
    grandma song,
Don't make me play that grandma song,
Don't make me play that grandma song
    again!

Douglas Mountain

Words by Arnold Sundgaard
Music by Alec Wilder

Cedars are growin' on Douglas Mountain,
Cedars are growin' so high;
Cedars are growin' on Douglas Mountain,
Joinin' the earth to the sky,
Joinin' the earth to the sky.

Snows are a-fallin' on Douglas Mountain,
Snows are a-fallin' so deep;
Snows are a-fallin' on Douglas Mountain,
Puttin' the bears to sleep,
Puttin' the bears to sleep.

Trimmin' the wicks on Douglas Mountain,
Shinin' my chimney so bright;
Trimmin' the wicks on Douglas Mountain,
So God can bring the night,
So God can bring the night.

Sun's goin' down on Douglas Mountain,
Nights are so long and so cold;
Sun's goin' down on Douglas Mountain,
And I am feelin' old,
And I am feelin' old.

Emmanuel

Words and Music by Michael W. Smith

Emmanuel, Emmanuel.
Wonderful Counselor,
Lord of life, Lord of all,
He's the Prince of Peace,
Mighty God, Holy One.
Emmanuel, Emmanuel.

Everywhere, Everywhere, Christmas Tonight

By Lewis H. Redner and Phillip Brooks

Christmas in lands of the fir tree and pine,
Christmas in lands of the palm tree and vine,
Christmas where snow peaks stand solemn and white,
Christmas where cornfields lie sunny and bright.
Ev'rywhere, ev'rywhere, Christmas tonight.

Christmas where children are hopeful and gay,
Christmas where old men are patient and gray,
Christmas where peace, like a dove in its flight,
Broods o'er brave men in the thick of the fight.
Ev'rywhere, ev'rywhere, Christmas tonight.

Feliz Navidad

Music and Lyrics by Jose Feliciano

Refrain:
Feliz Navidad.
Feliz Navidad.
Feliz Navidad.
Prospero año y felicidad.

Repeat Refrain

I want to wish you a Merry Christmas,
With lots of presents to make you happy.
I want to wish you a Merry Christmas
From the bottom of my heart.

I want to wish you a Merry Christmas,
With mistletoe and lots of cheer,
With lots of laughter throughout the years,
From the bottom of my heart.

Refrain

The First Noel

17th Century English Carol

Music from W. Sandys' *Christmas Carols*

The first Noel, the angel did say,
Was to certain poor shepherds in
    fields as they lay;
In fields where they lay keeping their sheep,
On a cold winter's night that was so deep.

Refrain:
Noel, Noel, Noel, Noel,
Born is the King of Israel.

They looked up and saw a star
Shining in the East, beyond them far;
And to the earth it gave great light,
And so it continued both day and night.

Refrain

And by the light of that same star,
Three wise men came from country far;
To seek for a King was their intent,
And to follow the star wherever it went.

Refrain

This star drew nigh to the northwest,
O'er Bethlehem it took its rest;
And there it did doth stop and stay,
Right over the place where Jesus lay.

Refrain

Then entered in those wise men three,
Full reverently upon their knee;
And offered there in His presence,
Their gold, and myrrh, and frankincense.

Refrain

Then let us all with one accord
Sing praises to our heav'nly Lord,
That hath made heav'n and earth of naught,
And with His blood mankind hath brought.

Refrain

The Friendly Beasts

Traditional English Carol

Jesus our brother, kind and good,
Was humbly born in a stable rude,
And the friendly beasts around Him stood,
Jesus our brother, kind and good.

"I," said the donkey, shaggy and brown,
"I carried His mother up hill and down;
I carried her safely to Bethlehem town."
"I," said the donkey, shaggy and brown.

"I," said the cow all white and red,
"I gave Him my manger for His bed;
I gave Him my hay to pillow His head."
"I," said the cow all white and red.

"I," said the sheep with curly horn,
"I gave Him my wool for His blanket warm;
He wore my coat on Christmas morn."
"I," said the sheep with curly horn.

"I," said the dove from the rafters high,
"I cooed Him to sleep so He would not cry;
We cooed Him to sleep, my mate and I."
"I," said the dove from the rafters high.

Thus every beast by some good spell,
In the stable dark was glad to tell
Of the gift he gave Emmanuel,
The gift he gave Emmanuel.

From Heaven Above to Earth I Come

Words and Music by Martin Luther

"From heav'n above to earth I come,
To bear good news to ev'ry home;
Glad tidings of great joy I bring,
Whereof I now will gladly sing.

"To you this night is born a Child
Of Mary, chosen mother mild;
This little Child of lowly birth
Shall be the joy of all the earth.

"'Tis Christ, our God, who far on high
Hath heard your sad and bitter cry;
Himself will your salvation be,
Himself from sin will make you free."

"He will on you the gifts bestow
Prepared by God for all below,
That in His kingdom, bright and fair,
You may with us His glory share.

"These are the tokens ye shall mark:
The swaddling-clothes and manger dark;
There ye shall find the Infant laid
By whom the heavens and earth
     were made."

Now let us all with gladsome cheer
Go with the shepherds and draw near
To see the precious gift of God,
Who hath His own dear Son bestowed.

Give heed, my heart, lift up thine eyes!
What is it in yon manger lies?
Who is this child, so young and fair?
The blessed Christ-child lieth there.

Welcome to earth, Thou noble Guest,
Through whom e'en wicked men are blest!
Thou coms't to share our misery;
What can we render, Lord, to Thee?

Ah, Lord, who hast created all,
How weak art Thou, how poor and small,
That Thou dost choose Thine infant bed
Where humble cattle lately fed!

Were earth a thousand times as fair,
Beset with gold and jewels rare,
It yet were far too poor to be
A narrow cradle, Lord, for Thee.

For velvets soft and silken stuff
Thou hast but hay and straw so rough,
Whereon Thou, King, so rich and great,
As 'twere Thy heaven, art throned in state.

And thus, dear Lord, it pleaseth Thee
To make this truth quite plain to me,
That all the world's wealth, honor, might,
Are naught and worthless in Thy sight.

Ah, dearest Jesus, Holy Child,
Make Thee a bed, soft, undefiled,
Within my heart, that it may be
A quiet chamber kept for Thee.

My heart for very joy doth leap,
My lips no more can silence keep;
I too must sing with joyful tongue
That sweetest ancient cradle-song:

Glory to God in highest heav'n,
Who unto us His Son hath giv'n!
While angels sing with pious mirth
A glad new year to all the earth.

From the Eastern Mountains

Traditional

From the eastern mountains,
Pressing on they come,
Wise men in their wisdom,
To His humble home.
Stirred by deep devotion,
Hasting from afar,
Ever journ'ing onward,
Guided by a star.

There their Lord and Savior
Meek and lowly lay,
Wondrous light that led them
Onward on their way.
Ever now to lighten
Nations from afar,
As they journey homeward
By that guiding star.

Thou who in a manger
Once hast lowly lain,
Who dost now in glory
O'er all kingdoms reign,
Gather in the heathen
Who in lands afar
Ne'er have seen the brightness
Of Thy guiding star.

Gather in the outcasts,
All who have astray,
Throw Thy radiance o'er them,
Guide them on their way.
Those who never knew Thee,
Those who have wandered far,
Guide them by the brightness
Of Thy guiding star.

Onward through the darkness
Of the lonely night,
Shining still before them
With Thy kindly light.
Guide them, Jew and Gentile,
Homeward from afar,
Young and old together,
By Thy guiding star.

Frosty the Snow Man

Words and Music by Steve Nelson and Jack Rollins

Frosty the snow man
Was a jolly, happy soul,
With a corncob pipe and
    a button nose
And two eyes made out of coal.
Frosty the snow man
Is a fairy tale, they say;
He was made of snow,
    but the children know
How he came to life one day.
There must have been some magic
In that old silk hat they found,
For when they placed it on his head,
He began to dance around.
Oh, Frosty the snow man
Was alive as he could be,
And the children say he could
    laugh and play
Just the same as you and me.

Frosty the snowman
Knew the sun was hot that day,
So he said, "Let's run and
    we'll have some fun
Now before I melt away."
Down to the village
With a broomstick in his hand,
Running here and there
    all around the square,
Sayin', "Catch me if you can."
He led them down the streets of town
Right to the traffic cop.
And he only paused a moment when
He heard him holler "Stop!"
For Frosty the snowman
Had to hurry on his way,
But he waved good-bye, sayin',
    "Don't you cry,
I'll be back again someday."

Thumpety thump thump,
Thumpety thump thump,
Look at Frosty go.
Thumpety thump thump,
Thumpety thump thump,
Over the hills of snow.

Fum, Fum, Fum

Traditional Catalonian Carol

On this joyful Christmas day
Sing fum, fum, fum.
On this joyful Christmas Day
Sing fum, fum, fum.
For a blessed Babe was born
Upon this day at break of morn.
In a manger poor and lowly
Lay the Son of God most holy.
Fum, fum, fum.

Thanks to God for holidays,
Sing fum, fum, fum.
Thanks to God for holidays,
Sing fum, fum, fum.
Now we all our voices raise
And sing a song of grateful praise,
Celebrate in song and story
All the wonders of His glory,
Fum, fum, fum.

Gesù Bambino

Text by Frederick H. Martens
Music by Pietro Yon

When blossoms flowered 'mid the snows,
Upon a winter night,
Was born the Child, the Christmas Rose,
The King of Love and Light.
The angels sang, the shepherds sang,
The grateful earth rejoiced,
And at His blessed birth
The stars their exultation voiced.

Refrain:
O come let us adore Him,
O come let us adore Him,
O come let us adore Him,
Christ the Lord.

Again the heart with rapture glows
To greet the holy night
That gave the world its Christmas Rose,
Its King of Love and Light.
Let ev'ry voice acclaim His name,
The grateful chorus swell,
From paradise to earth He came
That we with Him might dwell.

Refrain

Ah! O come let us adore Him,
Ah! Adore Him, Christ the Lord.
O come, o come, o come let us adore Him,
Let us adore Him, Christ the Lord.

The Gift

Words and Music by Tom Douglas and Jim Brickman

Female:
Winter snow is falling down,
Children laughing all around,
Lights are turning on,
Like a fairy tale come true.
Sitting by the fire we made,
You're the answer when I prayed
I would find someone
And baby, I found you.

All I want is to hold you forever.
All I need is you more every day.
You saved my heart from being
    broken apart.
You gave your love away,
And I'm thankful every day for the gift.

Male:
Watching as you softly sleep,
What I'd give if I could keep
Just this moment,
If only time stood still.
But the colors fade away,
And the years will make us gray,
But, baby, in my eyes,
    you'll still be beautiful.

Both:
All I want is to hold you forever.
All I need is you more every day.

Male:
You saved my heart from being
    broken apart.

Female:
You gave your love away.

Male:
And I'm thankful every day.

Both:
For the gift.

Both:
All I want is to hold you forever.
All I need is you more every day.

Male:
You saved my heart from being
    broken apart.

Female:
You gave your love away.

Male:
I can't find the words to say.

Female:
That I'm thankful every day.

Both:
For the gift.

Go Tell It on the Mountain

African-American Spiritual
Verses by John W. Work, Jr.

Refrain:
Go tell it on the mountain,
Over the hills and ev'rywhere;
Go tell it on the mountain
That Jesus Christ is born.

While shepherds kept their watching
O'er silent flocks by night,
Behold, throughout the heavens,
There shone a holy light.

Refrain

The shepherds feared and trembled
When, lo! above the earth
Rang out the angel chorus
That hailed our Savior's birth.

Refrain

Down in a lowly manger
The humble Christ was born,
And God sent us salvation
That blessed Christmas morn.

Refrain

God Bless Us Everyone

Music by Alan Menken
Lyrics by Lynn Ahrens

from the musical *A Christmas Carol*

Let the stars in the sky
Remind us of man's compassion.
Let us love 'til we die,
And God bless us, ev'ryone.

In your heart there's a light
As bright as a star in heaven.
Let it shine through the night,
And God bless us, ev'ryone.

Refrain:
'Til each child is fed,
'Til all men are free,
'Til the world becomes a fam'ly...

Star by star up above
And kindness by human kindness,
Light this world with your love,
And God bless us, ev'ryone.

Refrain

Let the stars in the sky
Remind us of man's compassion.
Let us love 'til we die,
And God bless us, ev'ryone.

God bless us, everyone.

God Rest Ye Merry, Gentlemen

19th Century English Carol

God rest ye merry, gentlemen,
Let nothing you dismay,
For Jesus Christ our Savior
Was born on upon this day,
To save us all from Satan's power
When we were gone astray.

Refrain:
O tidings of comfort and joy,
Comfort and joy;
O tidings of comfort and joy.

In Bethlehem, in Jewry,
This blessed Babe was born,
And laid within a manger
Upon this blessed morn;
To which His mother Mary
Did nothing take in scorn.

Refrain

From God our Heav'nly Father,
A blessed Angel came;
And unto certain shepherds
Brought tidings of the same;
How that in Bethlehem was born
The Son of God by Name.

Refrain

Goin' on a Sleighride

Words and Music by Ralph Blane

We've got the sleigh bells,
The winter season sleigh bells.
Hear those sleigh bells ringing
Merrily ev'rywhere we go.
We've got the horses,
The smartest team of horses,
'Cause they know their way back home
Through all the ice and snow.
We've got a comfort,
A fancy quilted comfort,
If we hit a little storm
It's gonna keep us warm.

Ev'rybody's goin',
Hearts are overflowin',
Start your harmonizin',
That's a full moon risin';

Why don't you come along?
We're goin' on a sleigh ride,
We're goin' on a sleigh ride,
And if you want to sing it's allowed.
So let your happiness hum along,
The moonlight isn't painted,
It helps you get acquainted
And starts you pairin' off from the crowd.

Later on while we skate around,
We'll build a fire and we'll wait around
Until a cozy corner can be found.
Then what'll we do?
I'll leave it to you,
We're gonna trust in that moon above,

And when the sleigh ride's over,
We're gonna be in clover,
After we cuddle near,
Maybe we'll find that we're in love.

Why don't you come along?
We're goin' on a sleigh ride,
We're goin' on a sleigh ride,
And if it starts to snow, let it snow.
So let your happiness hum along,
The moonlight isn't painted,
It helps you get acquainted
You'll steal a kiss without mistletoe.

Later on while we skate around,
We'll build a fire and we'll wait around
Until a cozy corner can be found.
Then what'll we do?
I'll leave it to you,
We're gonna trust in that moon above,
And when the sleigh ride's over,
We're gonna be in clover,
After we cuddle near,
Maybe we'll find that we're in love.

Good Christian Men, Rejoice

14th Century Latin Text
Translated by John Mason Neale
14th Century German Melody

Good Christian men, rejoice,
With heart and soul and voice;
Give ye heed to what we say:
News! News! Jesus Christ is born today!
Ox and ass before him bow,
And He is in the manger now;
Christ is born today!
Christ is born today!

Good Christian men, rejoice,
With heart and soul and voice;
Now ye hear of endless bliss;
Joy! Joy! Jesus Christ was born for this!
He has ope'd the heav'nly door,
And man is blessed evermore.
Christ was born for this!
Christ was born for this!

Good Christian men, rejoice,
With heart and soul and voice;
Now ye need not fear the grave;
Peace! Peace! Jesus Christ was born to save!
Calls you one and calls you all,
To gain His everlasting hall.
Christ was born to save!
Christ was born to save!

Going Home for Christmas

Words and Music by Steven Curtis Chapman and James Isaac Elliot

Her house was where
   the fam'ly gathered
Ev'ry Christmas Eve.
A feast was on the table
And gifts were placed beneath the tree.
Ev'rything was picture perfect.
Grandpa would laugh and say,
"That woman spends the whole year
Getting' ready for this day."

One year the leaves began to fall
And her health began to fail.
We moved her to a place where
They could watch her night and day.
But she kept making plans for Christmas
From her little room.
She told ev'ryone, "I'll miss you,
But I'll be leaving soon."

Refrain:
I'm goin' home for Christmas,
And I'm going home to stay.
I'm going home for Christmas
And nothing's gonna keep me away.

And I'll be with the ones I love
To celebrate the Savior's birth.
This gift will be worth more to me
Than anything on earth.
I'm goin' home, home for Christmas.

All the leaves outside have fallen
To be covered by the snow.
The fam'ly comes with food and gifts,
And Grandpa comes alone.
There's a sadness in our silence
As the Christmas story's read.
And with tears, Grandpa reminds us
Of the words that Grandma said.

Refrain

And she'll be face to face with Jesus,
As we celebrate His birth.
This gift will be worth more to her
Than anything on earth,
'Cause she'll be home, home for Christmas.

And as we sing "Joy to the World"
I can't help thinkin'
Of the joy that's shining in her eyes
    right now.
And though our hearts still ache,
We know that as we celebrate,
She's singing with the herald angels
And heaven's glowing on her face.

And now she's home,
    she's home for Christmas,
Oh, now she's home to stay.
Oh, she's home for Christmas;
Nothing could've kept her away.

Yeah, she'll be face to face with Jesus,
As we celebrate His birth.
And His gift will be worth more to her
Than anything on earth.
She's home, she's home for Christmas.
And she is home, she's home for Christmas.

Good King Wenceslas

Words by John M. Neale
Music from *Piae Cantiones*

Good King Wenceslas look'd out
On the feast of Stephen,
When the snow lay round about,
Deep and crisp and even;
Brightly shone the moon that night,
Though the frost was cruel,
When a poor man came in sight,
Gath'ring winter fuel.

"Hither, page, and stand by me,
If thou know'st it, telling,
Yonder peasant, who is he?
Where and what his dwelling?"
"Sire, he lives a good league hence,
Underneath the mountain;
Right against the forest fence,
By Saint Agnes' fountain."

"Bring me flesh and bring me wine,
Bring me pine logs hither;
Thou and I will see him dine,
When we bear them thither."
Page and monarch, forth they went,
Forth they went together;
Through the rude wind's wild lament
And the bitter weather.

"Sire, the night is darker now,
And the wind blows stronger;
Fails my heart, I know not how,
I can go no longer."
"Mark my footsteps, my good page;
Tread thou in them boldly:
Thou shalt find the winter's rage
Freeze thy blood less coldly."

In his master's steps he trod,
Where the snow lay dinted;
Heat was in the very sod
Which the saint had printed.
Therefore, Christian men, be sure,
Wealth or rank possessing,
Ye who now will bless the poor,
Shall yourselves find blessing.

Good News

Words and Music by Rob Mathes

Refrain:
Good news, good news.
An angel brings good news.
Good news, good news.
I meet you with good news.

Close your eyes, fold your hands,
For a moment let your sorrow fade.
Why, oh, why are you afraid?
Has this world stripped you of your faith?
Close your eyes and on bended knee
Listen to an angel pray
And once again prepare the way
So you'll see a gift that's given.
For you a time of joy;
Behold, a baby boy.

Refrain

Bow your head, speak not a word,
Let the silence take you far from here.
The spirit of a child dry ev'ry tear,
And may your doubts, they disappear.
Bow your head and on bended knee
Hear the story once again.
The child grew up to wear a cross,
A child grew up to pledge a life.
For us a time of joy;
Behold, Christ, a baby boy.

Refrain

For us is born this night
In a manger, wrapped in swaddling clothes,
Christ the Savior, Christmas day,
All our burdens washed away.
We break the bread, we pour the wine,
And angels descend with a heavenly sigh.

Refrain Twice

I leave you with good news.

Grandma Got Run Over by a Reindeer

Words and Music by Randy Brooks

Refrain:
Grandma got run over by a reindeer
Walking home from our house
    Christmas Eve.
You can say there's no such thing as Santa,
But as for me and Grandpa, we believe.

She'd been drinkin' too much eggnog
And we begged her not to go,
But she forgot her medication,
And she staggered out the door
    into the snow.
When we found her Christmas morning
At the scene of the attack,
She had hoofprints on her forehead
And incriminating Claus marks on her back.

Refrain

Now we're all so proud of Grandpa,
He's been taking this so well.
See him in there watching football,
Drinking beer and playing cards with
    Cousin Mel.
It's not Christmas without Grandma.
All the family's dressed in black,
And we just can't help but wonder:
Should we open up her gifts or
    send them back?

Refrain

Now the goose is on the table,
And the pudding made of fig,
And the blue and silver candles
That would just have matched the hair in
    Grandma's wig.
I've warned all my friends and neighbors,
Better watch out for yourselves.
They should never give a license
To a man who drives a sleigh and
    plays with elves.

Refrain

Grandma's Killer Fruitcake

Words and Music by Elmo Shropshire and Rita Abrams

The holidays were upon us
And things were goin' fine,
'Til the day I heard the doorbell
And a chill ran up my spine.
I grabbed the wife and children
As the postman wheeled it in;
A yearly Christmas nightmare
Had just come back again.

Refrain:
It was harder than the head
   of Uncle Bucky;
Heavy as a sermon of Preacher Lucky;
One's enough to give the whole state
   of Kentucky
A great big belly ache!
It was denser than a drove of
   barnyard turkeys;
Tougher than a truckload of all-beef jerky;
Drier than a drought in Albuquerque;
Grandma's killer fruitcake!

Now I had to swallow some marginal fare
At our fam'ly feast.
I even downed Aunt Dolly's possum pie
Just to keep the fam'ly peace.
I winced at Wilma's gizzard mousse,
But said it tasted fine.
But that lethal weapon Grandma baked
Is where I draw the line.

Refrain

It's early Christmas mornin';
The phone rings us awake.
It's Grandma, Pa, she wants to know
How we liked the cake.
Well, Grandma, I never...we couldn't...
It was unbelievable, that's for sure!
What's that you say?
Oh, no Grandma, please!
Don't send us anymore!

Refrain Twice

Man, that's killer fruit...
Grandma's killer fruitcake.
Grandma's killer fruitcake!

The Greatest Gift of All

Words and Music by John Jarvis

Dawn is slowly breaking,
Our friends have all gone home.
You and I are waiting
For Santa Claus to come.
There's a present by the tree,
Stockings on the wall.
Knowing you're in love with me
Is the greatest gift of all.

The fire is slowly fading,
Chill is in the air.
All the gifts are waiting
For children ev'rywhere.
Through the window I can see
Snow began to fall.
Knowing you're in love with me
Is the greatest gift of all.

Just before I go to sleep
I hear a church bell ring.
Merry Christmas ev'ryone
Is the song it sings.
So I say a silent prayer
For creatures great and small.
Peace on earth, goodwill to men,
Is the greatest gift of all.
Peace on earth, goodwill to men,
Is the greatest gift of all.

Greenwillow Christmas

By Frank Loesser

from the musical *Greenwillow*

Three wise men followed a star one night
To where glad bells were pealing,
And soon beheld the Holy Child
And all the shepherds kneeling.

Refrain:
Come see the star, come hear the bells.
Come learn the tale this night forever tells.
Come one and all from far and wide.
Come know the joy, the joy, the joy.
Come know the joy of Christmastide.

'Twas long ago in Bethlehem
Yet ever live the glory,
And hearts all glow and voices rise
A-caroling the story.

Refrain

Grown-Up Christmas List

Words and Music by David Foster and Linda Thompson-Jenner

Do you remember me?
I sat upon your knee.
I wrote to you with childhood fantasies.

Well I'm all grown-up now
And still need help somehow.
I'm not a child but my heart still can dream.
So here's my lifelong wish,
My grown-up Christmas list,
Not for myself, but for a world in need.

Refrain:
No more lives torn apart,
And wars would never start,
And time would heal all hearts.
And ev'ryone would have a friend,
And right would always win,
And love would never end.
This is my grown-up Christmas list.

As children we believed
The grandest sight to see
Was something lovely wrapped
   beneath our tree.
Well, heaven surely knows
That packages and bows
Can never heal a hurting human soul.

Refrain

What is this illusion called?
The innocence of youth.
Maybe only in our blind belief
Can we ever find the truth.

Refrain

This is my only lifelong wish.
This is my grown-up Christmas list.

The Happiest Christmas

Words by Miles Rudge
Music by Ted Dicks

The happiest Christmas is a homecoming Christmas,
With the snow flutt'ring down till the world seems new.
Bright candles burning, old friends returning,
The wishes of children coming true.
And the happiest wishes are just old-fashioned wishes:
May your days be merry, your sorrows be small.
May ones you love be near you;
That's the happiest Christmas of all.

Happy Birthday, Jesus

Words and Music by Lee Pockriss

Happy birthday, Jesus.
Happy birthday, Jesus.

Katy got a dolly that cries and blinks its eyes.
Jimmy got an automatic plane that really flies.
But we were poor that Christmas,
So Momma stayed up all night long,
Sittin' in the kitchen making us a present; it was this song.

Refrain:
Church bells ring-a-ling, angels sing-a-ling,
Happy birthday, Jesus.
Snowflakes ting-a-ling, sleigh bells jing-a-ling,
Happy birthday, Jesus.
All year long we wait
Just to celebrate this Christmas morn,
'Cause we want you to know
We're so glad you were born.
Oh, have a merry, very happy birthday, Jesus.

Teddy bears get broken and trains will rust away.
All the fancy playthings seem to fall apart one day.
But I was very lucky; when ev'rybody's gift was gone,
I still had my present; Momma's song of Christmas lived on and on.

Refrain

Spoken:
Christmas is for children, and now I have my own.
Their eyes are full of wonder when all the toys are shown.
But I'll give them something better than anything that's on TV,
Something very special, something made forever, [*sung*] this melody.

Refrain

Happy Christmas, Little Friend

Lyrics by Oscar Hammerstein II
Music by Richard Rodgers

The soft morning light of a pale winter sun
Is tracing the trees on the snow.
Leap up, little friend, and fly down the stairs
For Christmas is waiting below.
There's a tree in the room running over with stars
That twinkle and sing to your eyes.
And under the tree there are presents that say,
Unwrap me and get a surprise.

Refrain:
Happy Christmas, little friend,
May your heart be laughing all day.
May your joy be a dream you'll remember,
As the years roll along on their way.
As the years roll along on their way,
You'll be showing your own kid a tree.
Then at last, my friend, you'll know
How happy a Christmas can be,
How happy a Christmas can be.

Repeat Refrain

Happy Holiday

Words and Music by Irving Berlin

from the Motion Picture *Irving Berlin's Holiday Inn*

Happy holiday, happy holiday.
While the merry bells keep ringing,
May your ev'ry wish come true.
Happy holiday, happy holiday.
May the calendar keep bringing
Happy holidays to you.

Repeat

Happy New Year Darling

Music and lyrics by Carmen Lombardo and Johnny Marks

Ev'ry time I hear "Auld Lang Syne,"
What memories it brings!
Crowds that flow, paper horns that blow,
And ev'rybody sings:

Refrain:
Happy New Year, darling!
I give this toast to you.
Happy New Year, darling!
May all your dreams come true.
Let's always make believe
Each night is New Year's Eve.
Then we'll always find
Our troubles far behind.
New year's resolutions
Were made to break, they say,
But I'll keep my promise
To love you more each day.
Let's ring out the old year
And ring in the new
With happy New Year, darling, to you!

Refrain

Happy Xmas (War Is Over)

Words and Music by John Lennon and Yoko Ono

So this is Xmas
And what have you done?
Another year over,
And a new one just begun;
And so this is Xmas,
I hope you have fun,
The near and the dear ones,
The old and the young.

Refrain:
A merry, merry Xmas
And a happy New Year.
Let's hope it's a good one
Without any fear.

And so this is Xmas
For weak and for strong,
The rich and the poor ones,
The road is so long.
And so, happy Xmas
For black and for white,
For the yellow and red ones,
Let's stop all the fights.

Refrain

So this is Xmas
And what have we done?
Another year over,
And a new one just begun;
And so this is Xmas,
We hope you have fun,
The near and the dear ones,
The old and the young.

Refrain

War is over if you want it,
War is over now.

Hark! The Herald Angels Sing

Words by Charles Wesley
Altered by George Whitefield
Music by Felix Mendelssohn-Bartholdy
Arranged by William H. Cummings

Hark! the herald angels sing,
"Glory to the newborn King!
Peace on earth, and mercy mild,
God and sinners reconciled!"
Joyful, all ye nations, rise,
Join the triumph of the skies;
With th'angelic host proclaim,
"Christ is born in Bethlehem!"
Hark! the herald angels sing,
"Glory to the newborn King!"

Christ, by highest heav'n adored,
Christ the everlasting Lord;
Late in time behold Him come,
Offspring of the virgin womb.
Veiled in flesh, the Godhead see:
Hail, th'incarnate Deity;
Pleased, as man, with men to dwell,
Jesus, our Emmanuel!
Hark! the herald angels sing,
"Glory to the newborn King!"

Hail, the heav'n-born Prince of peace!
Hail, the Son of Righteousness!
Light and life to all He brings,
Ris'n with healing in his wings.
Mild He lays His glory by,
Born that man no more may die,
Born to raise the sons of earth,
Born to give them second birth.
Hark! the herald angels sing,
"Glory to the newborn King!"

He Is Born, the Holy Child
(Il est ne, le divin Enfant)

Traditional French Carol

Refrain:
He is born, the holy Child,
Play the oboe and bagpipes merrily!
He is born, the holy Child,
Sing we all of the Savior mild.

Through long ages of the past,
Prophets have betold His coming;
Through long ages of the past,
Now the time has come at last!

Refrain

O how lovely, o how pure
Is this perfect Child of heaven;
O how lovely, O how pure,
Gracious gift of God to man!

Refrain

Jesus, Lord of all the world,
Coming as a Child among us;
Jesus, Lord of all the world,
Grant to us Thy heav'nly peace.

Refrain

Here We Come A-Wassailing

Traditional

Here we come a-wassailing
Among the leaves so green,
Here we come a-wand'ring,
So fair to be seen.

Refrain:
Love and joy come to you,
And to your wassail too;
And God bless you and send you
A happy New Year,
And God send you
A happy New Year.

We are not daily beggars
That beg from door to door,
But we are neighbors' children,
Whom you have seen before.

Refrain

We have got a little purse
Of stretching leather skin;
We want a little money
To line it well within.

Refrain

God bless the master of this house,
Likewise the mistress too,
And all the little children
That round the table go.

Refrain

The Holly and the Ivy

18th Century English Carol

The holly and the ivy,
When they are both full grown,
Of all the trees that are in the wood,
The holly bears the crown.

Refrain:
The rising of the sun
And the running of the deer,
The playing of the merry organ,
Sweet singing in the choir.

The holly bears a blossom
As white as lily flow'r,
And Mary bore sweet Jesus Christ
To be our dear Savior.

Refrain

The holly bears a berry
As red as any blood,
And Mary bore sweet Jesus Christ
To do poor sinners good.

Refrain

The holly bears a prickle
As sharp as any thorn,
And Mary bore sweet Jesus Christ
On Christmas day in the morn.

Refrain

The holly bears a bark
As bitter as the gall,
And Mary bore sweet Jesus Christ
For to redeem us all.

Refrain

Repeat Verse 1

Refrain

THE LYRIC LIBRARY

A Holly Jolly Christmas

Music and Lyrics by Johnny Marks

Have a holly jolly Christmas,
It's the best time of the year.
I don't know if there'll be snow
But have a cup of cheer.

Have a holly jolly Christmas,
And when you walk down the street,
Say hello to friends you know
And ev'ryone you meet.

Oh, ho, the mistletoe
Hung where you can see,
Somebody waits for you,
Kiss her once for me.

Have a holly jolly Christmas,
And in case you didn't hear,
Oh, by golly, have a holly jolly
Christmas this year.

Repeat All

(There's No Place Like) Home for the Holidays

Words by Al Stillman
Music by Robert Allen

Refrain 1:
Oh, there's no place like home for the holidays,
'Cause no matter how far away you roam,
When you pine for the sunshine of a friendly gaze,
For the holidays you can't beat home, sweet home.

I met a man who lives in Tennessee,
And he was headin' for
Pennsylvania and some homemade pumpkin pie.
From Pennsylvania folks are trav'lin'
Down to Dixie's sunny shore;
From Atlantic to Pacific, gee,
The traffic is terrific!

Refrain 2:
Oh, there's no place like home for the holidays,
'Cause no matter how far away you roam,
If you want to be happy in a million ways,
For the holidays you can't beat home, sweet home.

Refrain 1

A home that knows your joy and laughter filled
With mem'ries by the score
Is a home you're glad to welcome with your heart.
From California to New England
Down to Dixie's sunny shore;
From Atlantic to Pacific, gee,
The traffic is terrific!

Refrain 2

How Brightly Beams the Morning Star

Words and Music by Philipp Nicolai
Translated by William Mercer

How brightly beams the morning star!
What sudden radiance from afar
Doth glad us with its shining?
The ray of God that breaks our night
And fills the darkened souls with light,
Who long for truth were pining.
Thy word, Jesus, truly feeds us,
Rightly leads us,
Life bestowing.
Praise, oh praise such love o'erflowing.

Through thee alone can we be blest;
Then deep be on our hearts imprest
The love that thou hast borne us;
So make us ready to fulfill
With burning seal thy holy will,
Though men may vex or scorn us;
Savior, let us never lose thee,
For we choose thee,
Thirst to know thee,
All are we and have we owe thee!

O praise to him who came to save,
Who conquer'd death and burst the grave;
Each day new praise resoundeth
To him the Lamb who once was slain,
The friend who none shall trust in vain,
Whose grace for ay aboundeth;
Sing, ye heavens, tell the story
Of his glory,
Till his praises
Flood with light earth's darkest places!

How Lovely Is Christmas

Words by Arnold Sundgaard
Music by Alec Wilder

How lovely is Christmas with boughs in the hall,
When bells ringle jingle and friends come to call.
How lovely is Christmas with joy on the wing,
While under your window the carolers sing,
"God rest ye, be merry, give peace where you may;
Remember the Child who was born on this day."
How lovely is Christmas, with songs in the air,
A bright merry Christmas, dear friends ev'rywhere.

How lovely is Christmas when children are near,
The sound of their laughter, sweet season of cheer.
How lovely is Christmas with gifts by the tree,
Each gift tells a story; oh, what will it be?
The yule log is burning, the stars gleam above,
Remember the gift of the Christ Child is love.
The bells ring for Christmas, our story now ends,
Goodnight, merry Christmas, dear neighbors and friends.

How lovely is Christmas with songs in the air,
A bright merry Christmas, dear friends ev'rywhere.

I Heard the Bells on Christmas Day

Words by Henry Wadsworth Longfellow
Music by John Baptiste Calkin

I heard the bells on Christmas day,
Their old familiar carols play,
And mild and sweet the words repeat,
Of peace on earth, goodwill to men.

I thought how as the day had come,
The belfries of all Christendom
Had rolled along th'unbroken song
Of peace on earth, goodwill to men.

And in despair I bowed my head:
"There is no peace on earth," I said,
"For hate is strong, and mocks the song
Of peace on earth, goodwill to men."

Then pealed the bells more loud and deep:
"God is not dead, nor doth He sleep;
The wrong shall fail, the right prevail,
With peace on earth, goodwill to men."

Till ringing, singing on its way,
The world revolved from night to day,
A voice, a chime, a chant sublime,
Of peace on earth, goodwill to men!

I Saw Mommy Kissing Santa Claus

Words and Music by Tommie Connor

I saw Mommy kissing Santa Claus
Underneath the mistletoe last night.
She didn't see me creep
Down the stairs to have a peep,
She thought that I was tucked up in my bedroom fast asleep.
Then I saw Mommy tickle Santa Claus,
Underneath his beard so snowy white.
Oh, what a laugh it would have been
If Daddy had only seen
Mommy kissing Santa Claus last night.

I Saw Three Ships

Traditional English Carol

I saw three ships come sailing in
On Christmas day, on Christmas day;
I saw three ships come sailing in
On Christmas day in the morning.

And what was in those ships all three
On Christmas day, on Christmas day?
And what was in those ships all three
On Christmas day in the morning?

Our Savior Christ and His lady
On Christmas day, on Christmas day.
Our Savior Christ and His lady
On Christmas day in the morning.

Pray, whither sailed those ships all three
On Christmas day, on Christmas day?
Pray, whither sailed those ships all three
On Christmas day, on Christmas day?

O, they sailed into Bethlehem
On Christmas day, on Christmas day;
O, they sailed into Bethlehem
On Christmas day in the morning.

And all the bells on earth shall ring
On Christmas day, on Christmas day;
And all the bells on earth shall ring
On Christmas day in the morning.

And all the angels in heav'n shall sing
On Christmas day, on Christmas day;
And all the angels in heav'n shall sing
On Christmas day in the morning.

And all the souls on earth shall sing
On Christmas day, on Christmas day;
And all the souls on earth shall sing
On Christmas day in the morning.

Then let us all rejoice amain
On Christmas day, on Christmas day;
Then let us all rejoice amain
On Christmas day in the morning!

I Wonder as I Wander

By John Jacob Niles

I wonder as I wander out under the sky,
How Jesus the Savior did come for to die.
For poor on'ry people like you and like I.
I wonder as I wander out under the sky.

When Mary birthed Jesus, 'twas in a cow's stall,
With wise men and farmers and shepherds and all.
But high from God's heaven a star's light did fall,
And the promise of ages it then did recall.

If Jesus had wanted for any wee thing,
A star in the sky or a bird on the wing,
Or all of God's angels in heav'n for to sing,
He surely could have it, 'cause He was the King.

Repeat Verse 1

I'll Be Home for Christmas

Words and Music by Kim Gannon and Walter Kent

I'm dreaming tonight of a place I love,
Even more than I usually do.
And although I know it's a long road back,
I promise you

I'll be home for Christmas,
You can count on me.
Please have snow and mistletoe
And presents on the tree.
Christmas Eve will find me
Where the lovelight gleams,
I'll be home for Christmas
If only in my dreams.

I'm Spending Christmas with You

Words and Music by Tom Occhipinti

The snow is gently falling,
The night is so cold.
The moon shines on the snow-covered trees.
And the road seemed like forever,
But I'm finally home.
We're alone on this Christmas Eve.

Refrain:
I'm spending Christmas with you.
It's the season when love is renewed.
My holiday wishes have already come true.
I'm spending Christmas with you.

The fireplace is burning,
And your hands feel so warm.
The presents are under our tree.
And I take you in my arms,
And your lips are touching mine.
And it feels like our first Christmas Eve.

Refrain

My holiday wishes have already come true.
I'm spending Christmas with you.

I've Got My Love to Keep Me Warm

Words and Music by Irving Berlin

from the 20th Century Fox Motion Picture *On the Avenue*

The snow is snowing,
The wind is blowing,
But I can weather the storm.
What do I care how much it may storm?
I've got my love to keep me warm.

I can't remember
A worse December;
Just watch those icicles form.
What do I care if icicles form?
I've got my love to keep me warm.

Off with my overcoat,
Off with my glove.
I need no overcoat,
I'm burning with love.

My heart's on fire,
The flame grows higher.
So I will weather the storm.
What do I care how much it may storm?
I've got my love to keep me warm.

Immanuel

Words and Music by Michael Card

A sign shall be given,
A virgin will conceive.
A human baby bearing
Undiminished Deity.
The glory of the nations,
A light for all to see;
And hope for all who will embrace
His warm reality.

Refrain:
Immanuel, our God is with us.
And if God is with us,
Who could stand against us?
Our God is with us, Immanuel.

For all those who live in the shadow of death,
A glorious light has dawned.
For all those who stumble in the darkness,
Behold, your light has come!

Refrain

So what will be your answer?
Oh, will you hear the call
Of Him who did not spare His son,
But gave Him for us all?
On earth there is no power,
There is no depth or height
Could ever separate us
From the love of God in Christ.

Refrain Twice

Infant Holy, Infant Lowly

Traditional Polish Carol
Paraphrased by Edith M.G. Reed

Infant holy, Infant lowly,
For His bed a cattle stall.
Oxen lowing, little knowing
Christ the Babe is Lord of all.
Swift are winging angels singing,
Noels ringing, tidings bringing:
Christ the Babe is Lord of all.

Flocks are sleeping, shepherds keeping
Vigil till the morning new,
Saw the glory, heard the story,
Tidings of a Gospel true.
Thus rejoicing, free from sorrow,
Praises voicing greet the morrow:
Christ the Babe was born for you.

Irish Carol

Traditional Irish Carol

Christmas Day is come; let's prepare for mirth,
Which fills the heav'ns and earth at this amazing birth.
Through both the joyous angels in strife and hurry fly,
With glory and hosannas, "All Holy" do they cry,
In heav'n the church triumphant adores with all her choirs,
The militant on earth with humble faith admires.

But why should we rejoice? Should we not rather mourn
To see the hope of nations thus in a stable born?
Where are his crown and scepter, where is His throne sublime,
Where is his throne majestic that should the stars outshine?
Is there no sumptuous palace, nor any inn at all
To lodge his heav'nly mother but in a filthy stall?

Oh! Cease, ye blessed angels, such clam'rous joys to make!
Though midnight silence favors, the shepherds are awake;
And you, o glorious star, that with new splendor brings,
From the remotest parts three learned eastern kings,
Turn somewhere else your luster, your rags elsewhere display,
For Herod may slay the babe, and Christ must straight away.

If we would then rejoice, let's cancel the old score,
And purposing amendment, resolve to sin no more;
For mirth can ne'er content us, without a conscience clear;
And thus we'll find true pleasure in all the usual cheer,
In dancing, sporting, rev'ling, with masquerade and drum,
So Christmas merry be, as Christians doth become.

It Came Upon the Midnight Clear

Words by Edmund H. Sears
Traditional English Melody
Adapted by Arthur Sullivan

It came upon the midnight clear,
That glorious song of old,
From angels bending near the earth
To touch their harps of gold:
"Peace on the earth, goodwill to men,
From heav'n's all-gracious King."
The world in solemn stillness lay
To hear the angels sing.

Still through the cloven skies they came
With peaceful wings unfurled,
And still their heavenly music floats
O'er all the weary world;
Above its sad and lowly plains,
They bend on hovering wing.
And ever o'er its Babel sounds
The blessed angels sing.

And ye, beneath life's crushing load,
Whose forms are bending low,
Who toil along the climbing way
With painful steps and slow,
Look now! For glad and golden hours
Come swiftly on the wing.
O rest beside the weary road,
And hear the angels sing.

For lo! The days are hastening on,
By prophet seen of old,
When, with the ever-circling years,
Shall come the time foretold
When peace shall over all the earth
Its ancient splendors fling,
And the whole world send back the song
Which now the angels sing.

It Must Have Been the Mistletoe
(Our First Christmas)

By Justin Wilde and Doug Konecky

It must have been the mistletoe,
The lazy fire, the falling snow,
The magic in the frosty air,
That feeling ev'rywhere.
It must have been the pretty lights
That glistened in the silent night,
Or maybe just the stars so bright
That shined above you.

Our first Christmas,
More than we'd been dreaming of.
Old Saint Nich'las had his fingers crossed
That we would fall in love.

It could have been the holiday,
The midnight ride upon a sleigh,
The countryside all dressed in white,
That crazy snowball fight.
It could have been the steeple bell
That wrapped us up within its spell.
It only took one kiss to know,
It must have been the mistletoe.

Our first Christmas,
More than we'd been dreaming of.
Old Saint Nich'las must have known that kiss
Would lead to all of this.

It must have been the mistletoe,
The lazy fire, the falling snow,
The magic in the frosty air,
That made me love you.
On Christmas Eve a wish came true,
That night I fell in love with you.
It only took one kiss to know,
It must have been the mistletoe.
It must have been the mistletoe.
It must have been the mistletoe.

It's Beginning to Look Like Christmas

By Meredith Willson

It's beginning to look a lot like Christmas,
Ev'rywhere you go.
Take a look in the five and ten,
Glistening once again,
With candy canes and silver lanes aglow.

It's beginning to look a lot like Christmas,
Toys in ev'ry store.
But the prettiest sight to see
Is the holly that will be
On your own front door.

A pair of hopalong boots
And a pistol that shoots
Is the wish of Barney and Ben;
Dolls that will talk
And will go for a walk
Is the hope of Janice and Jen;
And Mom and Dad can hardly wait
For school to start again.

It's beginning to look a lot like Christmas,
Ev'rywhere you go.
There's a tree in the Grand Hotel,
One in the park as well,
The sturdy kind that doesn't mind the snow.

It's beginning to look a lot like Christmas,
Soon the bells will start.
And the thing that will make them ring
Is the carol that you sing
Right within your heart.

It's Christmas in New York

Words and Music by Billy Butt

Church bells are ringing,
Choirs are singing,
Joy they are bringing,
It's Christmas in New York.
Streetlights are pleasing,
Snowflakes are teasing,
Central Park's freezing,
It's Christmas in New York.
The stars in the heavens are so bright
They tell of a baby that was born in night.

Rest'rant signs swaying,
Blue skies are graying,
Ev'ryone's saying,
It's Christmas in New York.
Skyscrapers gleaming,
Broadway lights beaming,
Children are dreaming,
It's Christmas in New York.
The lights on the Christmas tree are fine,
The sights of the shopping sprees, the gifts,
    yours and mine.

Stockings are filling,
Champagne is chilling,
It's all so thrilling,
It's Christmas in New York.
Log fires are burning,
Santa's returning
Feeling each yearning,
It's Christmas in New York.

Church bells are ringing,
Choirs are singing,
Joy they are bringing,
It's Christmas in New York,
It's Christmas in New York,
It's Christmas in New York.

It's Christmas Time All Over the World

Words and Music by Hugh Martin

It's Christmas time all over the world,
And Christmas here at home.
The church bells chime wherever we roam,
So "Joyeux Noël," "Feliz Natal," "Gellukkig Kerstfeest" to you!

The snow is thick in most of the world
And children's eyes are wide
As old Saint Nick gets ready to ride,
So "Feliz Navidad, "Cracium Fericit," and "Happy New Year" to you!

Though the customs may change,
And the language is strange,
This appeal we feel is real
In Holland or Hong Kong.

It's Christmas time all over the world,
In places near and far;
And so, my friends, wherever you are,
A "Fröhliche Weihnachten!" "Kala Christougena!" "Yoi Kurisumasu!"
Which means a very merry Christmas to you!

It's Just Another New Year's Eve

Lyric by Marty Panzer
Music by Barry Manilow

Don't look so sad.
It's not so bad, you know.
It's just another night,
That's all it is.
It's not the first.
It's not the worst, you know.
We've come through all the rest.
We'll get through this.

We've made mistakes,
But we've made good friends, too.
Remember all the nights
We've spent with them.
And all our plans,
Who says they can't come true?
Tonight's another chance
To start again.

Refrain:
It's just another New Year's Eve,
Another night like all the rest.
It's just another New Year's Eve,
Let's make it the best.
It's just another New Year's Eve
It's just another Auld Lang Syne.
But when we're through
This New Year you'll see
We'll be just fine.

We're not alone,
We've got the world, you know.
And it won't let us down,
Just wait and see.
And we'll grow old,
But think how wise we'll grow.
There's more, you know,
It's only New Year's Eve.

Refrain

Jesus Born on This Day

Words and Music by Mariah Carey and Walter Afanasieff

Today a child is born on earth.
(Today a child is born on earth.)
Today the glory of God
Shines ev'rywhere for all the world.

Refrain 1:
Oh, Jesus, born on this day,
He is our light and salvation.
Oh, Jesus, born on this day,
He is the King of all nations.

Behold the lamb of God has come.
(Behold the lamb of God has come.)
Behold the Savior is born.
Sing of His love to ev'ryone.

Refrain 2:
Oh, Jesus, born on this day,
Heavenly child in a manger.
Oh, Jesus, born on this day,
He is our Lord and Savior.

Today our hearts rejoice in Him.
(Today our hearts rejoice in Him.)
Today the light of His birth
Fills us with hope and brings peace on earth.

Refrain 1

Today a child is born on earth.
(Today a child is born on earth.)

Five Times:
He is light, He is love, He is grace,
Born on Christmas day.

Jingle-Bell Rock

Words and Music by Joe Beal and Jim Boothe

Jingle-bell, jingle-bell, jingle-bell rock,
Jingle-bells swing and jingle-bells ring.
Snowin' and blowin' up bushels of fun,
Now the jingle hop has begun.

Jingle-bell, jingle-bell, jingle-bell rock,
Jingle bells chime in jingle-bell time.
Dancin' and prancin' in Jingle Bell Square
In the frosty air.

What a bright time, it's the right time,
To rock the night away.
Jingle-bell time is a swell time
To go glidin' in a one-horse sleigh.

Giddy-ap jingle horse, pick up your feet,
Jingle around the clock.
Mix and mingle in a jinglin' beat,
That's the jingle-bell rock.

Jingle Bells

Words and Music by J. Pierpont

Dashing through the snow,
In a one-horse open sleigh,
O'er the fields we go,
Laughing all the way.
Bells on bobtail ring,
Making spirits bright,
What fun it is to ride and sing
A sleighing song tonight! Oh!

Refrain:
Jingle bells, jingle bells,
Jingle all the way.
Oh what fun it is to ride
In a one-horse open sleigh!
Jingle bells, jingle bells,
Jingle all the way.
Oh what fun it is to ride
In a one-horse open sleigh!

A day or two ago
I thought I'd take a ride,
And soon Miss Fanny Bright
Was seated by my side.
The horse was lean and lank,
Misfortune seemed his lot,
He got into a drifted bank
And we, we got upsot! Oh!

Refrain

Now the ground is white,
Go it while you're young.
And take the girls tonight
And sing this sleighing song.
Just get a bobtail bay,
Two-forty for his speed,
Then hitch him to an open sleigh
And crack, you'll take the lead! Oh!

Refrain

Jingle, Jingle, Jingle

Music and Lyrics by Johnny Marks

Jingle, jingle, jingle,
You will hear my sleigh bells ring.
I am old Kris Kringle,
I'm the king of jingling.
Jingle, jingle, reindeer,
Through the frosty air they'll go,
They are not just plain deer,
They're the fastest deer I know. (Ho! Ho!)
You must believe that on Christmas Eve
I won't pass you by,
I'll dash away in my magic sleigh,
Flying through the sky.
Jingle, jingle, jingle,
You will hear my sleigh bells ring.
I am old Kris Kringle
I'm the king of jingling. (Ho! Ho!)

Jingle, jingle, jingle,
You will hear his sleigh bells ring.
Jolly old Kris Kringle
Is the king of jingling.
Jingle, jingle, reindeer,
Through the frosty air they'll go,
They are not just plain deer,
They're the fastest deer I know. (Ho! Ho!)
You must believe that on Christmas Eve
He won't pass you by,
He'll dash away in his magic sleigh,
Flying through the sky.
Jingle, jingle, jingle,
You will hear his sleigh bells ring.
Jolly old Kris Kringle
Is the king of jingling. (Ho! Ho!)

Jolly Old St. Nicholas

Traditional 19th Century American Carol

Jolly old Saint Nicholas,
Lean your ear this way.
Don't you tell a single soul
What I'm going to say.
Christmas Eve is coming soon,
Now, you dear old man,
Whisper what you'll bring to me;
Tell me if you can.

When the clock is striking twelve,
When I'm fast asleep,
Down the chimney broad and black,
With your pack you'll creep.
All the stockings you will find
Hanging in a row.
Mine will be the shortest one,
You'll be sure to know.

Johnny wants a pair of skates;
Susy wants a sled;
Nellie wants a picture book,
Yellow, blue, and red;
Now I think I'll leave to you
What to give the rest.
Choose for me, dear Santa Claus,
You will know the best.

Joseph Dearest, Joseph Mine

Traditional German Carol

Joseph dearest, Joseph mine,
Help me cradle the Babe divine,
Sing to Him a lullaby:
"Now sleep and rest,
Your slumber blest,
O Jesus."

Refrain:
He came among us at Christmas time,
At Christmas time in Bethlehem,
Bringing all men far and wide
Love's Diadem.
Eia, eia.
Jesus Christ, who came to earth to save us.

Gladly, Mother Mary mine,
Will I rock the Babe divine,
While I sing a lullaby:
"O sleep and rest,
Your slumber blest,
O Jesus!"

Refrain

Joy to the World

Words by Isaac Watts
Music by George Frideric Handel
Arranged by Lowell Mason

Joy to the world! The Lord is come;
Let earth receive her King;
Let ev'ry heart prepare Him room,
And heav'n and nature sing,
And heav'n and nature sing,
And heav'n and heav'n and nature sing.

Joy to the earth! The Savior reigns;
Let men their songs employ;
While fields and floods, rocks, hills and plains
Repeat the sounding joy,
Repeat the sounding joy,
Repeat, repeat the sounding joy.

No more let sin and sorrows grow,
Nor thorns infest the ground;
He comes to make His blessings flow
Far as the curse is found,
Far as the curse is found,
Far as, far as the curse is found.

He rules the world with truth and grace,
And makes the nations prove
The glories of His righteousness
And wonders of His love,
And wonders of His love,
And wonders, wonders of His love.

Joyous Christmas

Music and Lyrics by Johnny Marks

Have a joyous Christmas, joyous Christmas,
Fill your heart with good cheer.
Thank the Lord above for all the love
You have from those you hold dear.

Refrain:
Let the Christmas bells ring out,
Proclaiming loud and clear:
Have a joyous Christmas, joyous Christmas,
And a happy New Year.

Have a joyous Christmas, joyous Christmas,
But don't fail to recall
That a tiny stranger in a manger
Was the start of it all.

Refrain

Have a joyous Christmas, joyous Christmas,
Sing it loudly and then
Pray for all your worth for peace on earth
And for goodwill to men.

Refrain

The Last Month of the Year
(What Month Was Jesus Born In?)

Words and Music by Vera Hall
Adapted and Arranged by Ruby Pickens Tartt and Alan Lomax

What month was my Jesus born in?
Last month of the year!
What month was my Jesus born in?
Last month of the year!

Refrain:
Oh, January, February, March,
April, May, June, oh Lord,
You got July, August, September,
October, and a November,
On the twenty-fifth day of December
In the last month of the year.

Well, they laid him in a manger,
Last month of the year!
Well, they laid him in a manger,
Last month of the year!

Refrain

Wrapped Him up in swaddling clothing,
Last month of the year!
Wrapped Him up in swaddling clothing,
Last month of the year!

Refrain

Well, He was born of the Virgin Mary,
Last month of the year!
He was born of the Virgin Mary,
Last month of the year!

Refrain

Let It Snow! Let It Snow! Let It Snow!

Words by Sammy Cahn
Music by Jule Styne

Oh, the weather outside is frightful,
But the fire is so delightful,
And since we've no place to go,
Let it snow! Let it snow! Let it snow!

It doesn't show signs of stopping,
And I brought some corn for popping,
The lights are turned way down low,
Let it snow! Let it snow! Let it snow!

When we finally kiss goodnight,
How I'll hate going out in the storm!
But if you'll really hold me tight,
All the way home I'll be warm.

The fire is slowly dying
And, my dear, we're still good-bye-ing,
But as long as you love me so,
Let it snow! Let it snow! Let it snow!

Let's Have an Old Fashioned Christmas

Lyric by Larry Conley
Music by Joe Solomon

Another year has rolled around,
In spite of ev'rything;
So let's make use of one excuse
To love and laugh and sing:

Refrain:
Let's have an old-fashioned Christmas,
Dress up an old-fashioned tree;
Let's make the spirit of Auld Lang Syne
The same as it used to be;
Hearts will be light as a feather
After some old-fashioned cheer;
So let's all be good fellows together,
Let's have an old-fashioned Christmas this year.

Repeat Refrain

Little Saint Nick

Words and Music by Brian Wilson and Mike Love

Merry Christmas, Saint Nick.
Ooh.

Well, way up north where the air gets cold,
There's a tale about Christmas that you've all been told.
And a real famous cat all dressed up in red,
And he spends his whole year workin' out on his sled.

Refrain:
It's the little Saint Nick (little Saint Nick).
It's the little Saint Nick (little Saint Nick).

Just a little bobsled, we call it Old Saint Nick,
And she'll walk a toboggan with a four-speed stick.
She's a candy-apple red with a ski for a wheel,
And when Santa gives her gas, man, just watch her peel.

Refrain

Run, run, reindeer.
Run, run, reindeer.
Oh, run, run, reindeer.
Run, run, reindeer.
He don't miss no one.

And haulin' through the snow at a fright'nin' speed
With a half a dozen deer with Rudy to lead.
He's gotta wear his goggles 'cause the snow really flies,
And he's cruisin' ev'ry pad with a little surprise.

Refrain

Lo, How a Rose E'er Blooming

15th Century German Carol
Translated by Theodore Baker
Music from *Alte Catholische Geistliche Kirchengesang*

Lo, how a rose e'er blooming
From tender stem hath sprung!
Of Jesse's lineage coming
As men of old have sung.
It came, a flow'ret bright,
Amid the cold of winter,
When half spent was the night.

Isaiah 'twas foretold it,
The Rose I have in mind,
With Mary we behold it,
The Virgin Mother kind.
To show God's love aright,
She bore to men a Savior,
When half spent was the night.

Love Came Down at Christmas

Text by Christina Rossetti
Traditional Irish Melody

Love came down at Christmas,
Love all lovely, love divine;
Love was born at Christmas,
Star and angels gave the sign.

Worship we the Godhead,
Love incarnate, love divine;
Worship we our Jesus,
But wherewith for sacred sign?

Love shall be our token;
Love be yours and love be mine,
Love to God and neighbor,
Love for plea and gift and sign.

Love Has Come

Words and Music by Amy Grant, Shane Keister and Michael W. Smith

Hurry now, wake up your eyes,
Time for little ones to see;
Daddy's got a big surprise
Hiding there beneath the Christmas tree.
How they are like the child in me.
See the wonder in their eyes,
Like a fairytale come true;
One more time I realize
All the love our lives have found in you.

Refrain:
Love has come
For the world to know,
As the wise men knew
Such a long time ago.
And I believe that angels sang
That hope had begun
When the God of glory,
Who is full of mercy,
Sent His Son.

If I could have a special dream
Coming true on Christmas morn,
I would want the world to see
How His Father smiled when Christ was born,
The greatest gift the world has known.
So come on, kids, look high and low
For all the toys you've dreamed to find,
But I believe you'll never know
A greater joy than Jesus' love inside.

Refrain

A Marshmallow World

Words by Carl Sigman
Music by Peter De Rose

It's a marshmallow world in the winter
When the snow comes to cover the ground.
It's the time for play, it's a whipped cream day,
I wait for it the whole year round.

Those are marshmallow clouds being friendly,
In the arms of the evergreen trees.
And the sun is red like a pumpkin head,
It's shining so your nose won't freeze.

The world is your snowball; see how it grows.
That's how it goes, whenever it snows.
The world is your snowball: just for a song,
Get out and roll it along.

It's a yum-yummy world made for sweethearts,
Take a walk with your favorite girl.
It's a sugar date, what if spring is late?
In winter it's a marshmallow world.

Mary, Did You Know?

Words and Music by Mark Lowry and Buddy Greene

Mary, did you know that your baby boy
Would one day walk on water?
Mary, did you know that your baby boy
Would save our sons and daughters?
Did you know that your baby boy
Has come to make you new;
This child that you delivered
Will soon deliver you?

Mary, did you know that your baby boy
Will give sight to the blind man?
Mary, did you know that your baby boy
Would calm a storm with His hand?
Did you know that your baby boy
Has walked where angels trod,
And when you kiss your little baby
You've kissed the face of God?

Oh, Mary, did you know?
Oh, Mary, did you know?
The blind will see, the deaf will hear,
The dead will live again,
The lame will leap, the dumb will speak
The praises of the Lamb?

Mary, did you know that your baby boy
Is Lord of all creation?
Mary, did you know that your baby boy
Will one day rule the nations?
Did you know that your baby boy
Was Heaven's perfect Lamb,
And the sleeping Child you're holding
Is the Great I Am?

Masters in This Hall

Traditional English

Masters in this hall,
Hear ye news today,
Brought from over sea,
And ever you I pray.

Refrain:
Nowell, nowell, nowell!
Nowell sing we clear!
Holpen are all folk on earth
Born is God's Son, so dear.
Nowell, nowell, nowell!
Nowell sing we loud!
God today hath all folk raised
And cast a-down the proud.

This is Christ, the Lord,
Masters be ye glad!
Christmas is come in,
And no folk shall be sad.

Refrain

Merry Christmas, Darling

Words and Music by Richard Carpenter and Frank Pooler

Greeting cards have all been sent,
The Christmas rush is through,
But I still have one more wish to make,
A special one for you.

Merry Christmas, darling,
We're apart, that's true;
But I can dream and in my dreams,
I'm Christmas-ing with you.

Holidays are joyful,
There's always something new.
But ev'ry day's a holiday
When I'm near to you.

Refrain:
The lights on my tree
I wish you could see,
I wish it ev'ry day.
The logs on the fire
Fill me with desire
To see you and to say
That I wish you a merry Christmas,
Happy New Year too.
I've just one wish on this Christmas Eve;
I wish I were with you.

Refrain

I wish I were with you.

The Merry Christmas Polka

Words by Paul Francis Webster
Music by Sonny Burke

They're tuning up the fiddles now,
The fiddles now, the fiddles now,
There's wine to warm the middles now
And set your head awhirl.

Around and round the room we go,
The room we go, the room we go,
Around and round the room we go,
So get yourself a girl.

Now ev'ry heart will start to tingle,
When sleigh bells jingle on Santa's sleigh,
Together we will greet Kris Kringle
And another Christmas day.

Refrain:
Come on and dance the merry Christmas polka,
Let ev'ryone be happy and gay.
Oh, it's the time to be jolly and deck the halls with holly,
So let's have a jolly holiday!
Come on and dance the merry Christmas polka,
Another joyous season has begun.
Roll out the yuletide barrels and sing out the carols,
A merry Christmas ev'ryone!

Refrain

Mister Santa

Words and Music by Pat Ballard

Mister Santa, bring me some toys,
Bring Merry Christmas to all girls and boys.
And ev'ry night I'll go to bed singing
And dream about the presents you'll be bringing.
Santa, promise me, please,
Give ev'ry reindeer a hug and a squeeze.
I'll be good, as good as can be,
Mister Santa, don't forget me.

Mister Santa, dear old Saint Nick,
Be awful careful and please don't get sick.
Put on your coat when breezes are blowin',
And when you cross the street, look where you're goin'.
Santa, we (I) love you so,
We (I) hope you never get lost in the snow.
Take your time when you unpack,
Mister Santa, don't hurry back.

Mister Santa, we've been so good,
We've watched the dishes and done what we should.
Made up the beds and scrubbed up our toesies,
We've used Kleenex when we've blown our nosies.
Santa, look at our ears,
They're clean as whistles, we're sharper than shears.
Now we've put you on the spot,
Mister Santa, bring us a lot.

Most of All I Wish You Were Here

Music and Lyrics by Denise Osso

Your gift arrived the first day it snowed.
I laid it under the tree.
I lit a fire, thinking about
How much you've given me.
I thought about how lucky we are
Though we're so far apart.
And when I wrapped up my present to you,
What I really gave you was my heart.

Refrain:
I wish you well, my love, on this Christmas day
And on ev'ry day of the year.
I miss you so. I guess you know
That most of all I wish you were here.

I've sent my cards and trimmed the tree,
Made a snowman too.
But Christmas is just another day
When I'm not with you.
I pray we'll be together again
Just like we used to be.
I send you my love. You can keep it 'til then,
When you come home to me.

Merry Christmas, oh my dear.
God keep you safe from harm.
When you come home I'll still be here
To hold you in my arms.

Refrain

Most of all I wish you were here.

The Most Wonderful Day of the Year

Music and Lyrics by Johnny Marks

We're on the island of Misfit Toys,
Here we don't want to stay.
We want to travel with Santa Claus,
In his magic sleigh.

Refrain:
A packful of toys means a sackful of joys
For millions of girls and for
   millions of boys
When Christmas day is here,
The most wonderful day of the year!

A jack-in-the-box waits for
   children to shout,
"Wake up, don't you know
   that it's time to come out!"
When Christmas day is here,
The most wonderful day of the year!
Toys galore, scattered on the floor,
There's no room for more,
And it's all because of Santa Claus!
A scooter for Jimmy, a dolly for Sue,
The kind that will even say
   "How do ya do"!
When Christmas day is here,
The most wonderful day of the year.

Refrain

It won't seem like Christmas till
   Dad gets his tie,
"It's just what I wanted" is his yearly cry.
When Christmas day is here,
The most wonderful day of the year.
Spirits gay, ev'ryone will say
Happy holiday
And the best to you the whole year through.
An electric train hidden high on the shelf
That Daddy gives David but then
   runs himself.
When Christmas day is here,
The most wonderful, wonderful,
   wonderful, wonderful,
Wonderful day of the year.

The Most Wonderful Time of the Year

Words and Music by Eddie Pola and George Wyle

It's the most wonderful time of the year,
With the kids jingle belling and ev'ryone telling,
"You be of good cheer."
It's the most wonderful time of the year.

It's the hap-happiest season of all,
With those holiday greetings and gay happy meetings
When friends come to call.
It's the hap-happiest season of all.

There'll be parties for hosting,
Marshmallows for toasting,
And caroling out in the snow.
There'll be scary ghost stories
And tales of the glories
Of Christmases long, long ago.

It's the most wonderful time of the year.
There'll be much mistltoe-ing, and hearts will be glowing
When loved ones are near.
It's the most wonderful time of the year.

It's the most wonderful time of the year.
There'll be much mistltoe-ing, and hearts will be glowing
When loved ones are near.
It's the most wonderful time,
It's the most wonderful time,
It's the most wonderful time of the year.

My Favorite Things

Lyrics by Oscar Hammerstein II
Music by Richard Rodgers

from the musical *The Sound of Music*

Raindrops on roses and whiskers on kittens.
Bright copper kettles and warm woolen mittens.
Brown paper packages tied up with strings,
These are a few of my favorite things.

Cream-colored ponies and crisp apple strudels,
Doorbells and sleigh-bells and schnitzel with noodles,
Wild geese that fly with the moon on their wings,
These are a few of my favorite things.

Girls in white dresses with blue satin sashes,
Snowflakes that stay on my nose and eyelashes,
Silver white winters that melt into springs,
These are a few of my favorites things.

When the dog bites,
When the bees stings,
When I'm feeling sad,
I simply remember my favorite things
And then I don't feel so bad!

The Night Before Christmas Song

Music by Johnny Marks
Lyrics adapted by Johnny Marks from Clement Moore's Poem

'Twas the night before Christmas and all through the house,
Not a creature was stirring, not even a mouse.
All the stockings were hung by the chimney with care,
In the hope that Saint Nicholas soon would be there.
Then what to my wondering eyes should appear,
A miniature sleigh and eight tiny reindeer,
A little old driver so lively and quick,
I knew in a moment it must be Saint Nick.
And more rapid than eagles his reindeer all came,
As he shouted, "On Dasher" and each reindeer's name.

And so up to the housetop the reindeer soon flew,
With the sleigh full of toys and Saint Nicholas too.
Down the chimney he came with a leap and a bound.
He was dressed all in fur and his belly was round.
He spoke not a word but went straight to his work,
And filled all the stockings, then turned with a jerk,
And laying his finger aside of his nose,
Then giving a nod, up the chimney he rose.
But I heard him exclaim as he drove out of sight,
"Merry Christmas to all, and to all a good night!"

THE LYRIC LIBRARY

Not That Far from Bethlehem

Words and Music by Jeff Borders, Gayla Borders and Lowell Alexander

Underneath the stars,
Just a simple man and wife.
Somewhere in the dark,
His words cut the silent night:
"Take my hand, for the Child
That you carry is God's own.
And though it seems the road is long,
We're not that far from Bethlehem,
Where all our hope and joy began.
For in our arms we'll cherish Him.
We're not that far from Bethlehem."

Let us celebrate
As the Christmases go by,
Learn to live our days
With our hearts near to the Child;
Ever drawn, ever close
To the only love that lasts.
And though two thousand years have passed,
We're not that far from Bethlehem,
Where all our hope and joy began.
For when our hearts still cherish Him,
We're not that far,
We're not that far from Bethlehem,
Where all our hope and joy began.
For when our hearts still cherish Him,
We're not that far,
We're not that far from Bethlehem.

Nuttin' for Christmas

Words and Music by Roy Bennett and Sid Tepper

I broke my bat on Johnny's head;
Somebody snitched on me.
I hid a frog in sister's bed;
Somebody snitched on me.
I spilled some ink on Mommy's rug,
I made Tommy eat a bug,
Bought some gum with a penny slug;
Somebody snitched on me.

Refrain:
Oh, I'm gettin' nuttin' for Christmas.
Mommy and Daddy are mad.
I'm gettin' nuttin' for Christmas,
'Cause I ain't been nuttin' but bad.

I put a tack on teacher's chair;
Somebody snitched on me.
I tied a knot in Susie's hair;
Somebody snitched on me.
I did a dance on Mommy's plants,
Climbed a tree and tore my pants,
Filled the sugar bowl with ants;
Somebody snitched on me.

Refrain

I won't be seeing Santa Claus;
Somebody snitched on me.
He won't come visit me because
Somebody snitched on me.
Next year I'll be going straight,
Next year I'll be good, just wait,
I'd start now, but it's too late;
Somebody snitched on me.

Refrain

So you better be good, whatever you do,
'Cause if you're bad I'm warning you,
You'll get nuttin' for Christmas.

O Christmas Tree

Traditional German Carol

O Christmas tree, o Christmas tree,
You stand in verdant beauty!
O Christmas tree, o Christmas tree,
You stand in verdant beauty!
Your boughs are green in summer's glow,
And do not fade in winter's snow.
O Christmas tree, o Christmas tree,
You stand in verdant beauty!

O Christmas tree, o Christmas tree,
Much pleasure doth thou bring me!
O Christmas tree, o Christmas tree,
Much pleasure doth thou bring me!
For ev'ry year the Christmas tree
Brings to us all both joy and glee.
O Christmas tree, o Christmas tree,
Much pleasure doth thou bring me!

O Christmas tree, O Christmas tree,
Thy candles shine out brightly!
O Christmas tree, O Christmas tree,
Thy candles shine out brightly!
Each bough doth hold its tiny light
That makes each toy to sparkle bright.
O Christmas tree, O Christmas tree,
Thy candles shine out brightly!

O Come, All Ye Faithful (Adeste Fidelis)

Words and Music by John Francis Wade
Latin Words translated by Frederick Oakeley

O come, all ye faithful, joyful and triumphant,
O come ye, o come ye to Bethlehem.
Come and behold Him, born the King of angels.

Refrain:
O come let us adore Him,
O come let us adore Him,
O come let us adore Him,
Christ the Lord.

Sing choirs of angels, sing in exultation,
Sing, all ye citizens of heaven above.
Glory to God in the highest.

Refrain

Yea, Lord, we greet Thee, born this happy morning.
Jesus, to Thee be all glory giv'n.
Word of the Father, now in flesh appearing.

Refrain

O Come, Little Children

Words by C. von Schmidt
Music by J.P.A. Schulz

O come, little children, from cot and from hall,
O come to the manger in Bethlehem's stall.
There meekly he lieth, the heavenly Child,
So poor and so humble, so sweet and so mild.

Now "Glory to God" sing the angels on high,
And "Peace upon earth" heav'nly voices reply.
Then come, little children, and join in the day
That gladdened the world on that first Christmas day.

O Come, O Come, Emmanuel

Plainsong, 13th Century
Words translated by John M. Neale and Henry S. Coffin

O come, o come, Emmanuel,
And ransom captive Israel,
That mourns in lonely exile here
Until the Son of God appear.

Refrain:
Rejoice, rejoice!
Emmanuel shall come to Thee, o Israel!

O come, Thou Dayspring, come and cheer
Our spirits by Thine advent here;
Disperse the gloomy clouds of night,
And death's dark shadows put to flight

Refrain

O come, Thou Wisdom, from on high,
And order all things far and nigh;
To us the path of knowledge show,
And cause us in her ways to go.

Refrain

O come, desire of nations, bind
All people in one heart and mind;
Bid envy, strife, and quarrels cease;
Fill the whole world with heaven's peace.

Refrain

O come, Thou Key of David, come,
And open wide our heav'nly home.
Make safe the way that leads on high,
And close the path to misery.

Refrain

O Hearken Ye

Lyric by Wihla Hutson
Music by Alfred Burt

O hearken ye who would believe,
The gracious tidings now receive:
Gloria, gloria,
In excelsis Deo.
The mighty Lord of heav'n and earth,
Today is come to human birth.
Gloria, gloria,
In excelsis Deo.

O hearken ye who long for peace,
Your troubled searching now may cease.
Gloria, gloria
In excelsis Deo.
For at his cradle you shall find
God's healing grace for all mankind.
Gloria, gloria,
In excelsis Deo.

O hearken ye who long for love,
And turn your hearts to God above.
Gloria, gloria,
In excelsis Deo.
The angel's song the wonder tells:
Now Love Incarnate with us dwells!
Gloria, gloria,
In excelsis Deo.

O Holy Night

French Words by Placide Cappeau
English Words by John S. Dwight
Music by Adolphe Adam

O holy night, the stars are brightly shining,
It is the night of the dear Savior's birth;
Long lay the world in sin and error pining,
Till He appeared and the soul felt its worth.
A thrill of hope, the weary world rejoices,
For yonder breaks a new and glorious morn;
Fall on your knees! O, hear the angel voices!
O night divine, o night when Christ was born!
O night, o holy night, o night divine!

Truly He taught us to love one another,
His law is love, and His gospel is peace;
Chains shall He break, for the slave is our brother,
And in His name all oppression shall cease.
Sweet hymns of joy in grateful chorus raise we,
Let all within us praise His holy name;
Christ is the Lord, o praise his name forever!
His pow'r and glory ever more proclaim!
His pow'r and glory ever more proclaim!

O Little Town of Bethlehem

Words by Phillips Brooks
Music by Lewis H. Redner

O little town of Bethlehem,
How still we see thee lie!
Above thy deep and dreamless sleep
The silent stars go by.
Yet in thy dark streets shineth
The everlasting light.
The hopes and fears of all the years
Are met in thee tonight.

For Christ is born of Mary,
And gathered all above,
While mortals sleep, the angels keep
Their watch of wond'ring love.
O morning stars, together
Proclaim the holy birth!
And praises sing to God the King,
And peace to men on earth!

How silently, how silently
The wondrous gift is giv'n!
So God imparts to human hearts
The blessings of His heav'n.
No ear may hear His coming,
But in this world of sin,
Where meek souls will receive Him still,
The dear Christ enters in.

O holy Child of Bethlehem,
Descend to us, we pray;
Cast out our sin and enter in;
Be born in us today.
We hear the Christmas angels
The great glad tidings tell;
O come to us, abide with us,
Our Lord Emmanuel!

O Sanctissima

Sicilian Carol

Oh, how joyfully,
Oh, how merrily
Christmas comes with its grace divine!
Grace again is beaming,
Christ the world redeeming;
Hail ye Christians,
Hail the joyous Christmas time!

Day of holiness,
Peace and happiness,
Joyful, glorious Christmas day!
Angels tell the story
Of this day of glory,
Praise Christ, our Saviour,
Born this Christmas day!

An Old Fashioned Christmas

Music and Lyrics by Johnny Marks

Let's have an old fashioned Christmas
With holly on the door
And a bright Christmas tree for the whole family,
With presents all over the floor.
We'll sing the old fav'rite carols
When neighbors come to call.
Let's have an old fashioned Christmas,
And a merry Christmas to all!

Old Toy Trains

Words and Music by Roger Miller

Old toy trains, little toy tracks,
Little toy drums comin' from a sack,
Carried by a man dressed in white and red.
Little boy, don't you think it's time you were in bed?
Close your eyes, listen to the skies,
All is calm, all is well;
Soon you'll hear Kris Kringle and the jingle bell

Bringin' little toy trains, little toy tracks,
Little toy drums comin' from a sack,
Carried by a man dressed in white and red
Little boy, don't you think it's time you were in bed?
So close your eyes, listen to the skies,
All is calm, all is well;
Soon you'll hear Kris Kringle and the jingle bell

Bringin' little toy trains, little toy tracks,
Little toy drums comin' from a sack,
Carried by a man dressed in white and red.
Little boy, don't you think it's time you were in bed?

On Christmas Night

Sussex Carol

On Christmas night true Christians sing,
To hear the news the angels bring,
On Christmas night true Christians sing,
To hear the news the angels bring,
News of great joy and of great mirth,
Tidings of our dear Savior's birth.

The King of Kings to us is giv'n,
The Lord of earth and King of heav'n;
The King of Kings to us is giv'n,
The Lord of earth and King of heav'n;
Angels and men with joy may sing
Of blest Jesus, their newborn King.

So how on earth can men be sad,
When Jesus comes to make us glad?
So how on earth can men be sad,
When Jesus comes to make us glad?
From all our sins to set us free,
Buying for us our liberty.

From out of darkness we have light,
Which makes the Angels sing this night;
From out of darkness we have light,
Which makes the Angels sing this night:
"Glory to God, His peace to men,
And goodwill, evermore! Amen."

Once in Royal David's City

Words by Cecil F. Alexander
Music by Henry J. Gauntlett

Once in royal David's city
Stood a lowly cattle shed,
Where a mother laid her Baby
In a manger for His bed.
Mary was that mother mild,
Jesus Christ her little child.

He came down to earth from heaven,
Who is God and Lord of all,
And His shelter was a stable,
And His cradle was a stall.
With the poor, and mean, and lowly,
Lived on earth our Savior holy.

Jesus is our childhood's pattern,
Day by day like us He grew;
He was little, weak and helpless,
Tears and smiles like us He knew.
And He feeleth for our sadness,
And He shareth in our gladness.

And our eyes at last shall see Him,
Through His own redeeming love,
For that child so dear and gentle
Is our Lord in heav'n above.
And He leads His children on
To the place where He is gone.

One Bright Star

Words and Music by John Jarvis

Long long ago in a world dark and cold,
A night so still, winter's chill,
One bright star was shining.
On a bed made of hay in a manger He lay.
The shepherds came, they knew His name,
King of Kings. A brand new day,
They saw the light in the darkness.
It shines on love and tenderness,
Brings out the hope that's in all of us.
May it shine its light on you this Christmas night.

On this Christmas day, may that star light your way.
This Christmas Eve, I still believe that same star still shines on me.
I saw the light in the darkness.
It shines on love and tenderness,
Brings out the hope that's in all of us.
May it shine its light on you this Christmas night.
May it shine its light on you this Christmas night.

One Small Child

Words and Music by David Meece

One small child in a land of a thousand,
One small dream of a Savior tonight.
One small hand reaching out to the starlight,
One small city of life, one small city of life.

One king bringing his gold and riches,
One king ruling an army of might,
One king kneeling with incense and candlelight,
One king bringing us life. Oh.
See Him lying, a cradle beneath Him,
See Him smiling in the stall.
See His mother praising His Father,
See His tiny eyelids fall.

One small light from the flame of a candle,
One small light from a city of might,
One small light from the stars in the endless night,
One small light from His face. Oh.
See the shepherds kneeling before Him,
See the kings on bended knee,
See the mother praising His Father,
See the blessed infant sleep.

One small child in a land of a thousand,
One small dream in a people of might.
One small hand reaching out to the starlight,
One small Savior of life, one small Savior of life.

Parade of the Wooden Soldiers

English Lyrics by Ballard MacDonald
Music by Leon Jessel

The toy shop door is locked up tight
And ev'rything is quiet for the night,
When suddenly the clock strikes twelve,
The fun's begun.

The dolls are in their best arrayed,
There's going to be a wonderful parade.
Hark to the drum, oh, here they come,
Cries ev'ryone.

Hear them all cheering,
Now they are nearing,
There's the captain stiff as starch.
Bayonets flashing,
Music is crashing,
As the wooden soldiers march.
Sabers a-clinking,
Soldiers a-winking,
At each pretty little maid.
Here they come!
Here they come!
Here they come!
Here they come!
Wooden soldiers on parade.

Daylight is creeping,
Dollies are sleeping,
In the toy shop window fast;
Soldiers so jolly
Think of each dolly,
Dreaming of the night that's past;
When in the morning,
Without a warning,
Toy man pulls the window shade.
There's no sign the wood brigade
Was ever put upon parade.

Pat-A-Pan

Words and Music by Bernard de la Monnoye

Willie, take your little drum,
Robin, bring your whistle, come.
When we hear the fife and drum,
Tu-re-lu-re-lu, pat-a-pat-a-pan.
When we hear the fife and drum,
Christmas should be light and fun.

Thus the men of olden days
Gave the King of Kings their praise.
When they hear the fife and drum,
Tu-re-lu-re-lu, pat-a-pat-a-pan.
With the drums they sing and play,
Full of joy on Christmas day.

God and man are now become
Closely joined as fife and drum.
When we play the fife and drum,
Tu-re-lu-re-lu, pat-a-pat-a-pan.
When on fife and drum we play,
Dance and make the holiday.

Pine Cones and Holly Berries
(It's Beginning to Look Like Christmas)

By Meredith Willson

from the musical *Here's Love*

Pine cones and holly berries,
Popcorn for you, apples for me.
Red striped candy, nutcracker handy,
Kettle a-bubblin', holiday tea.
Snow clouds hang low and threat'nin',
Maybe it won't, prayin' it may.
The brightest fireplace glows in ev'ry face,
Waiting for Christmas Day.

There'll be walk-a-round songs
And talk-a-round songs,
Songs of the inn and stable.
There'll be morningtime songs
And eveningtime songs
And grace at ev'ry table.
And jingle bells will jingle
All the way all day.

It's beginning to look a lot like Christmas,
Ev'rywhere you go;
There's a tree in the Grand Hotel,
One in the park as well,
The sturdy kind that doesn't mind the snow.
It's beginning to look a lot like Christmas,
Soon the bells will start;
And the thing that will make them ring
Is the carol that you sing
Right within your heart,
Right within your heart.

A Place Called Home

Music by Alan Menken
Lyrics by Lynn Ahrens

from the musical *A Christmas Carol*

There's a place called home I can almost see,
With a red front door and a roaring fire and a Christmas tree.
It's a place called home, full of love and family,
And I'm there at the door watching you come home to me.

Refrain:
Through the years, I'll recall this day,
In your arms, when I fin'lly found my way
To a place called home and a life with you,
Where the days are long and the love is strong and the dreams are true.

Just a place called home you and I will always see.
In the dark of the night let your heart come to me,
To the place in my heart where you're always home with me.

Refrain

Just a place called home that my heart will always see.
In the dark of the night let your heart come to me,
To the place in my heart where you're always home with me.

Precious Promise

Words and Music by Steven Curtis Chapman

Oh what a precious promise,
Oh, what a gift of love;
An angel tells a virgin that
She's gonna have a son.
And though it's a precious promise,
She wonders how can this be?
What will the people say
And what if Joseph can't believe?
And her questions and her fears
Are met with an overwhelming joy
That God has chosen her.
Oh, what a precious promise;
Mary waits as heaven comes to earth.

Oh what a precious promise,
Oh, what a gift of love.
Joseph makes his choice to do
What few men would have done:
To take Mary as his bride
When she's already carrying a child
That isn't his own.
Oh what a precious promise;
Mary and the child will have a home.

And shepherds stand on a hillside,
Their hearts racing with the news
  the angel told them.
A star's light fills up the dark sky
As the night of precious promise
  is unfolding.

Oh, what a precious promise,
Oh, what a gift of love.
The waiting now is over
And the time has fin'lly come
For the God who made this world
To roll back the curtain and unveil
His passion for the heart of man.
Oh, what a precious promise;
Lying in a manger in Bethlehem.
Oh, what a precious promise,
Lying in a manger in Bethlehem.

Pretty Paper

Words and Music by Willie Nelson

Crowded streets, busy feet hustle by him.
Downtown shoppers, Christmas is night.
There he sits all alone on the sidewalk.
Hoping that you won't pass him by.

Should you stop? Better not,
Much too busy. You're in a hurry.
My how time does fly.
In the distance the ringing of laughter,
And in the midst of the laughter he cries.

Refrain:
Pretty paper, pretty ribbons of blue.
Wrap your presents to your darling from you.
Pretty pencils to write, "I love you."
Pretty paper, pretty ribbons of blue.

Repeat Refrain

Ring Out, Ye Wild and Merry Bells

Words and Music by C. Maitland

Ring out, ye wild and merry bells,
Ring out the old, old story
That first was told by angel tongues
From out the realms of glory.
Peace on earth was their sweet song,
Glory in the highest!
Echoing all the hills away,
Glory in the highest!

Refrain:
Ring, sweet bells, ring evermore,
Peal from ev'ry steeple.
Christ, the Lord, shall be our God
And we shall be His people!

Ring out, ye silv'ry bells, ring out,
Ring out your exultation
That God with man is reconciled.
Go tell it to the nations.
Therefore let us all today,
Glory in the highest!
Banish sorrow far away,
Glory in the highest!

Refrain

Rise Up, Shepherd, and Follow

African-American Spiritual

There's a star in the east on Christmas morn,
Rise up, shepherd, and follow.
It will lead to the place where the Savior's born,
Rise up, shepherd, and follow.

Refrain:
Leave your ewes and leave your lambs,
Rise up, shepherd, and follow.
Leave your sheep and leave your rams,
Rise up, shepherd, and follow.
Follow, follow,
Rise up, shepherd, and follow.
Follow the star of Bethlehem,
Rise up, shepherd, and follow.

If you take good heed to the angel's word,
Rise up, shepherd, and follow.
You'll forget all your flocks, you'll forget your herd,
Rise up, shepherd, and follow.

Refrain

Rockin' Around the Christmas Tree

Music and Lyrics by Johnny Marks

Rockin' around the Christmas tree
At the Christmas party hop.
Mistletoe hung where you can see,
Ev'ry couple tries to stop.

Rockin' around the Christmas tree,
Let the Christmas spirit ring.
Later we'll have some pun'kin pie
And we'll do some caroling.

You will get a sentimental feeling when you hear
Voices singing "Let's be jolly,
Deck the halls with boughs of holly!"

Rockin' around the Christmas tree.
Have a happy holiday.
Ev'ryone dancing merrily
In the new old-fashioned way.

Rocking

Traditional Czech Carol

Baby Jesus, gently sleep, do not stir;
We will bring a coat of fur.
We will rock you, rock you, rock you,
Gently slumber as we rock you,
See the fur to keep you warm,
Snugly fits your tiny form.

Mary's precious baby sleep, gently sleep,
Sleep in comfort, slumber deep.
We will rock you, rock you, rock you,
Gently slumber as we rock you,
We will praise you all we can,
Darling, darling little man.

Rudolph, the Red-Nosed Reindeer

Music and Lyrics by Johnny Marks

from the film *Rudolph the Red-Nosed Reindeer: The Movie*

You know Dasher and Dancer and Prancer and Vixen,
Comet and Cupid and Donner and Blitzen,
But do you recall
The most famous reindeer of all?

Rudolph, the red-nosed reindeer
Had a very shiny nose,
And, if you ever saw it,
You would even say it glows.
All of the other reindeer
Used to laugh and call him names,
They never let poor Rudolph
Join in any reindeer games.
Then one foggy Christmas Eve
Santa came to say,
"Rudolph, with your nose so bright,
Won't you guide my sleigh tonight?"
Then how the reindeer loved him
As they shouted out with glee:
"Rudolph, the red-nosed reindeer,
You'll go down in history!"

Santa Baby

By Joan Javits, Phil Springer and Tony Springer

Mister Claus, I feel as though I know ya,
So you won't mind if I should get familya,
   will ya?

Santa baby, slip a sable under the tree
   for me.
I've been an awful good girl, Santa baby,
So hurry down the chimney tonight.

Santa baby, a fifty-four convertible, too,
   light blue.
I'll wait up for you, dear Santa baby,
So hurry down the chimney tonight.

Think of all the fun I've missed.
Think of all the fellas that I haven't kissed.
Next year I could be just as good
If you check off my Christmas list.

Santa baby, I want a yacht and really that's
   not a lot.
Been an angel all year, Santa baby,
So hurry down the chimney tonight.

Santa baby, one little thing I really do need,
The deed to a platinum mine, Santa honey,
So hurry down the chimney tonight.

Santa cutie, and fill my stocking with a
   duplex and cheques.
Sign your X on the line, Santa cutie,
And hurry down the chimney tonight.

Come and trim my Christmas tree
With some decorations bought at Tiffany.
I really do believe in you.
Let's see if you believe in me.

Santa baby, forgot to mention one little thing,
   a ring!
I don't mean a phone, Santa baby,
So hurry down the chimney tonight.

Santa, Bring My Baby Back (To Me)

Words and Music by Claude DeMetruis and Aaron Schroeder

Don't need a lot of presents
To make my Christmas bright.
I just need my baby's arms
Wound around me tight.

Refrain:
Oh, Santa, hear my plea.
Santa, bring my baby back to me.

The Christmas tree is ready,
The candles all aglow,
But with my baby far away
What good is mistletoe?

Refrain

Please make those reindeer hurry;
The time is drawin' near.
It sure won't seem like Christmas
Unless my baby's here.

Don't fill my sock with candy,
No bright and shiny toy.
You wanna make me happy
And fill my heart with joy,

Then, Santa, hear my plea.
Santa, bring my baby back to me.

The Santa Claus Parade

Music and Lyrics by Johnny Marks

There's a happy celebration
In each town across the nation
At the Santa Claus Parade.
All the grown-ups and the kiddies
In the towns and in the cities
Love the Santa Claus Parade.
Dasher, Dancer, Prancer, Vixen,
Comet, Cupid, Donner, Blitzen,
Rudolph leads the whole brigade.
When you hear all the cheering
You will see Santa nearing
At the Santa Claus Parade.

Clowns come tumbling all along the way
As ev'ry band begins to play:
"To all a happy holiday."
And when you see the presents loaded in the sleigh,
You'll know that Christmas isn't very far away.

Repeat Verse 1

Shake Me I Rattle (Squeeze Me I Cry)

Words and Music by Hal Hackady and Charles Naylor

I was passing by a toy shop on the corner of the square,
Where a little girl was looking in the window there.
She was looking at a dolly in a dress of rosy red.
And around the pretty dolly hung a little sign that said:

Refrain:
Shake me I rattle, squeeze me I cry
As I stood there beside her I could hear her sigh.
Shake me I rattle, squeeze me I cry.
Please take me home and love me.

I recalled another toy shop on a square so long ago
Where I saw a little dolly that I wanted so.
I remembered, I remembered how I longed to make it mine.
And around that other dolly hung another little sign:

Refrain

It was late and snow was following as the shoppers hurried by,
Past the girlie at the window with her little head held high.
They were closing up the toy shop as I hurried through the door.
Just in time to buy the dolly that her heart was longing for.

Refrain

Silent Night

Words by Joseph Mohr
Translated by John F. Young
Music by Franz X. Gruber

Silent night, holy night!
All is calm, all is bright.
Round yon Virgin Mother and Child.
Holy Infant so tender and mild,
Sleep in heavenly peace,
Sleep in heavenly peace.

Silent night, holy night!
Shepherds quake at the sight.
Glories stream from heaven afar,
Heavenly hosts sing Alleluia,
Christ the Savior is born!
Christ the Savior is born.

Silent night, holy night!
Son of God, love's pure light.
Radiant beams from thy holy face
With the dawn of redeeming grace,
Jesus Lord at Thy birth.
Jesus Lord at Thy birth.

Silver and Gold

Music and Lyrics by Johnny Marks

Silver and gold, silver and gold,
Ev'ryone wishes for silver and gold,
How do you measure its worth?
Just by the pleasure it gives here on earth?

Silver and gold, silver and gold,
Mean so much more when I see
Silver and gold decorations
On ev'ry Christmas tree.

Silver Bells

Words and Music by Jay Livingston and Ray Evans

from the Paramount Picture *The Lemon Drop Kid*

Christmas makes you feel emotional.
It may bring parties or thoughts devotional.
Whatever happens or what may be,
Here is what Christmastime means to me.

City sidewalks, busy sidewalks,
Dressed in holiday style;
In the air there's a feeling of Christmas.
Children laughing, people passing,
Meeting smile after smile,
And on ev'ry street corner you hear:

Refrain:
Silver bells, silver bells,
It's Christmastime in the city.
Ring-a-ling, hear them ring,
Soon it will be Christmas day.

Strings of street lights, even stoplights
Blink a bright red and green
As the shoppers rush home with their treasures.
Hear the snow crunch, see the kids bunch,
This is Santa's big scene,
And above all this bustle you hear:

Refrain

The Sleep of the Infant Jesus

Traditional French Carol

Here, 'mid the ass and oxen mild,
Sleep, sleep, sleep, thou tiny child.

Refrain:
Thousand cherubim, thousand seraphim,
Guarding o'er the bed of the great Lord of love.

Here, 'mid the rose and lily bright,
Sleep, sleep, sleep, thou tiny child.

Refrain

Here, 'mid the shepherds' glad delight,
Sleep, sleep, sleep, thou tiny child.

Refrain

The Snow Lay on the Ground

Traditional Irish Carol

The snow lay on the ground, the star shone bright,
When Christ our Lord was born on Christmas night.
Venite adoremus Dominum;
Venite adoremus Dominum.

Refrain:
Venite adoremus Dominum;
Venite adoremus Dominum.

'Twas Mary, Virgin pure, of holy Anne,
That brought into this world the God made man.
She laid Him in a stall at Bethlehem,
The ass and oxen share the night with them.

Refrain

Saint Joseph, too, was by to tend the Child;
To guard Him and protect His Mother mild;
The Angels hovered round and sang this song:
Venite adoremus Dominum.

Refrain

Snowfall

Lyrics by Ruth Thornhill
Music by Claude Thornhill

Snowfall, softly, gently drift down.
Snowflakes whisper 'neath my window.
Cov'ring trees misty white,
Velvet breeze 'round my doorstep.
Gently, softly, silent snowfall!

Some Children See Him

Lyric by Wihla Hutson
Music by Alfred Burt

Some children see Him lily white,
The Baby Jesus born this night.
Some children see Him lily white,
With tresses soft and fair.

Some children see Him bronzed and brown,
The Lord of heav'n to earth come down;
Some children see Him bronzed and brown,
With dark and heavy hair.

Some children see Him almond-eyed,
This Savior whom we kneel beside,
Some children see Him almond-eyed,
With skin of yellow hue.

Some children see Him dark as they,
Sweet Mary's Son to whom we pray;
Some children see Him dark as they,
And, ah, they love Him too!

The children in each diff'rent place
Will see the Baby Jesus' face
Like theirs, but bright with heav'nly grace,
And filled with holy light.

O lay aside each earthly thing,
And with thy heart as offering,
Come worship now the Infant King,
'Tis love that's born tonight!

Some Things for Christmas
(A Snake, Some Mice, Some Glue and a Hole Too)

Lyric by Jacquelyn Reinach and Joan Lamport
Music by Jacquelyn Reinach

I want a snake for Christmas,
All slip'pry and slimy and red;
I'll take that snake for Christmas and make
A nice home in my sister's bed!

I want some mice for Christmas,
As frisky and quick as can be;
Won't it be nice to uncage those mice,
When Mommy has ladies to tea!

I want some glue, there's lots I can do,
With a little bit of glue and a shoe!
I'm not asking much for Christmas,
Just a snake and some mice and some glue;
Just some mice and a snake
And some glue sure would make my dreams come true!

I could use some worms for Christmas,
All ooey and gooey and wet;
Think of the squirms when Dad sees those worms,
In a dish of meatballs and spaghet'!

And, if you please, if you purty, purty please,
For my brother's dungarees send me fleas!
I'm not asking for much for Christmas,
Just a snake and some mice and some glue;
And some worms and some fleas,
Just a few things like these'd make my dreams come true!

I want a hole for Christmas,
A hole that is deep as it's wide;
When mommy finds out what this song's about,
Then I'll have a good place to hide.

Standing in the Rain

Words and Music by Sydney Carter

Refrain:
Standing in the rain,
Knocking on the window,
Knocking on the window
   on a Christmas day.
There he is again,
Knocking on the window,
Knocking on the window in the same
   old way.

No use knocking on the window,
There is nothing we can do, sir.
All the beds are booked already,
There is nothing left for you, sir.

Refrain

No use knocking on the window;
Some are lucky, some are not, sir.
We are Christian men and women,
But we're keeping what we've got, sir.

Refrain

No, we haven't got a manger,
No, we haven't got a stable.
We are Christian men and women
Always willing, never able.

Standing in the rain,
Knocking on the window,
Knocking on the window
   on a Christmas day.

Jesus Christ has gone to heaven,
One day he'll be coming back, sir.
In this house he will be welcome.
But we hope he won't be black, sir.

Refrain

Standing in the rain.

The Star Carol

Lyric by Wihla Hutson
Music by Alfred Burt

Long years ago on a deep winter night,
High in the heav'ns a star shone bright,
While in a manger a wee Infant lay,
Sweetly asleep on a bed of hay.

Jesus, the Lord, was that Baby so small,
Laid down to sleep in a humble stall;
Then came the star and it stood overhead,
Shedding its light 'round His little bed.

Dear Baby Jesus, how tiny Thou art,
I'll make a place for Thee in my heart,
And when the stars in the heavens I see,
Ever and always I think of Thee.

The Star Carol (Canzone d'i Zampognari)

English Lyric and Music Adaptation by Peter Seeger
(Based on a Traditional Neapolitan Carol)

'Twas on a night like this,
A little Babe was born;
The shepherds gathered 'round
To guard Him till the dawn.

Above them shown a star,
A star so wond'rous light;
Never since in all these years
Have we seen one half so bright.

Shining so truly, shining so brightly,
Guiding their footsteps from afar.
It led them through the night,
A path to love and brotherhood
By following its light.

Oh, come with us tonight,
And join us on our way;
For we have found that star once more
To greet a better day.

For though throughout our land
Men search the skies in vain,
Yet turn their glance within their hearts
They would find this star again.

Shining so truly, shining so brightly,
Guiding our footsteps from afar.
It leads us through the night,
A path to love and brotherhood
By following its light.

Still Her Little Child

Words and Music by Ray Boltz and Steve Millikan

When she laid Him in the manger,
He was still her little child.
In a city filled with strangers,
He was still her little child.
Though the inn was full and the night
    was cold,
She held Him close and smiled.
When she laid Him in a manger,
He was still her little child.

When the angels called Him Savior,
He was still her little child.
When the wise men gave Him treasure,
He was still her little child.
When the shepherds bowed before Him,
A star shone all the while.
And when the angel called Him Savior,
He was still her little child.

And when He grew in strength and wisdom,
He was still her little child.
And when He spoke, the people listened;
But He was still her little child.
And when He healed the lame and dying,
They would follow Him for miles.
And when He grew in strength and wisdom,
He was still her little child.

And when the people turned against Him,
He was still her little child.
When they shouted, "Crucify Him,"
He was still her little child.
And when they nailed Him to a
    wooden cross,
Then we were reconciled.
When she held His broken body,
He was still her little child.
He was still her little child.

Still, Still, Still

19th Century Salzburg Melody
Traditional Austrian Text

Still, still, still,
To sleep is now His will.
On Mary's breast He rests in slumber
While we pray in endless number.
Still, still, still,
To sleep is now his will.

Sleep, sleep, sleep,
While we Thy vigil keep.
And angels come from heaven singing
Songs of jubilation bringing
Sleep, sleep, sleep,
While we thy vigil keep.
Sleep, sleep, sleep,
While we thy vigil keep.

A Strange Way to Save the World

Words and Music by Dave Clark, Mark Harris and Don Koch

I'm sure he must have been surprised
At where this road had taken him.
'Cause never in a million lives
Would he have dreamed of Bethlehem.
And, standing at the manger,
He saw with his own eyes
The message from the angel come to life.
And Joseph said,

Refrain:
"Why me? I'm just a simple man of trade.
Why Him, with all the rulers in the world?
Why here inside this stable filled with hay?
Why her? She's just an ordinary girl."
Now I'm not one to second-guess
What angels have to say,
But this is such a strange way to save the world.

To think of how it could have been
If Jesus had come as He deserved.
There would have been no Bethlehem,
No lowly shepherds at His birth.
But Joseph knew the reason
Love had to reach so far.
And as he held the Savior in his arms,
He must have thought,

Refrain

Now I'm not one to second-guess
What angels have to say,
But this is such a strange way to save the world.
This is such a strange way, such a strange way,
A strange way to save the world.

Suzy Snowflake

Words and Music by Sid Tepper and Roy Bennett

Here comes Suzy Snowflake,
Dressed in a snow white gown,
Tap, tap, tappin' at your windowpane
To tell you she's in town.

Here comes Suzy Snowflake,
Soon you will hear her say:
"Come out ev'ryone and play with me;
I haven't long to stay.

If you wanna make a snowman,
I'll help you make one, one, two, three.
If you wanna take a sleigh ride,
The ride's on me."

Here comes Suzy Snowflake,
Look at her tumblin' down,
Bringing joy to ev'ry girl and boy;
Suzy's come to town.

Tennessee Christmas

Words and Music by Amy Grant and Gary Chapman

Come on, weather man,
Give us a forecast snowy white.
Can't you hear the prayers
Of every childlike heart tonight?
Rockies are callin', Denver snow falling.
Somebody said it's four feet deep.
But it doesn't matter, give me the laughter
I'm gonna choose to keep

Refrain:
Another tender Tennessee Christmas.
The only Christmas for me.
Where the love circles around us
Like the gifts around our tree.

Well, I know there's more snow up
    in Colorado
Than my roof will ever see.
But a tender Tennessee Christmas
Is the only Christmas for me.

Ev'ry now and then I get
A wanderin' urge to see.
Maybe California,
Maybe Tinsel Town's for me.
There's a parade there, we'd have it
    made there.
Bring home a tan for New Year's Eve.
Sure sounds exciting, awfully inviting,
Still I think I'm gonna keep

Refrain

Well, they say in L.A. it's a warm holiday,
It's the only place to be.
But a tender Tennessee Christmas
Is the only Christmas for me.
A tender Tennessee Christmas
Is the only Christmas for me.

That Christmas Feeling

Words and Music by Bennie Benjamin and George Weiss

How I love that Christmas feeling;
How I treasure its friendly glow.
See the way a stranger greets you
Just as though you'd met him Christmases ago.

Christmas helps you to remember
To do what other folks hold dear.
What a blessed place the world would be
If we had that Christmas feeling all year.

There Is No Christmas Like a Home Christmas

Words by Carl Sigman
Music by Mickey J. Addy

There is no Christmas like a home Christmas
With your dad and mother, sis and brother there,
With their hearts humming at your homecoming,
And that merry yuletide spirit in the air.

Christmas bells, Christmas bells,
Ringing loud and strong.
Follow them, follow them,
You've been away too long.
There is no Christmas like a home Christmas
For that's the time of year all roads lead home.

There's a Song in the Air

Words and Music by Josiah G. Holland and Karl P. Harrington

There's a song in the air! There's a star in the sky!
There's a mother's deep prayer and a baby's low cry!
And the star rains its fire while the beautiful sing,
For the manger of Bethlehem cradles a King!

There's a tumult of joy o'er the wonderful birth,
For the virgin's sweet boy is the Lord of the earth.
Ay! The star rains its fire while the beautiful sing,
For the manger of Bethlehem cradles a King!

In the light of that star lie the ages impearled;
And that song from afar has swept over the world.
Ev'ry hearth is aflame, and the beautiful sing
In the homes of the nations that Jesus is King!

We rejoice in the light, and we echo the song
That comes down through the night from the heavenly throng.
Ay! We shout to the lovely evangel they bring,
And we greet in His cradle our Savior and King!

This Is Christmas (Bright, Bright the Holly Berries)

Lyric by Wihla Hutson
Music by Alfred Burn

Bright, bright the holly berries
In the wreath upon the door,
Bright, bright the happy faces
With the thoughts of joys in store.
White, white the snowy meadow
Wrapped in slumber deep and sweet,
White, white the mistletoe
'Neath which two lovers meet.

Refrain:
This is Christmas,
This is Christmas,
This is Christmas time.

Gay, gay the children's voices
Filled with laughter, filled with glee,
Gay, gay the tinseled things
Upon the dark and spicy tree.
Day, day when all mankind
May hear the angel's song again,
Day, day when Christ was born
To bless the sons of men.

Refrain

Sing, sing ye heav'nly host
To tell the blessed Savior's birth,
Sing, sing in holy joy,
Ye dwellers all upon the earth.
King, King yet tiny Babe
Come down to us from God above,
King, King of ev'ry heart
Which opens wide to love.

Refrain

This Baby

Words and Music by Steven Curtis Chapman

What child is this, who, laid to rest,
On Mary's lap is sleeping?
Whom angels greet with anthems sweet,
While shepherds watch are keeping?

Well, he cried when he was hungry,
Did all the things that babies do.
He rocked and he napped on his mother's lap,
And he wiggled and giggled and cooed.
There were the cheers when he took his first step
And the tears when he got his first teeth.
Almost ev'rything about this little baby
Seemed as natural as it could be.

Refrain:
But this baby made the angels sing,
And this baby made a new star shine in the sky.
This baby had come to change the world.
This baby was God's own son.
This baby was like no other one.
This baby was God with us.
This baby was Jesus.

And this baby grew into a young boy.
Who learned to read and write and wrestle with Dad.
There was the climbing of trees and the scraping of knees
And all fun that a boy's born to have.
He grew taller and some things started changing,
Like his complexion and the sound of his voice.
There was work to be done as a carpenter's son,
And all the neighbors said he's such a fine boy.

But this boy made the angels sing,
And this boy made a new star shine in the sky.
This boy had come to change the world.
This boy was God's own son,
This boy was like no other one.
This boy was God with us.
This boy became a man.

Love made him laugh, death made him cry,
But the life that he lived and the death that he died,
He showed us heaven with his hands and his heart,
'Cause this man was God's own son.
This man was like no other one.
Holy and pure right from the start.

But this baby made the angels sing,
And this baby made a new star shine in the sky.
This baby had come to change the world.
This baby was God's own son.
This baby was like no other one.
This baby was God with us.
This baby, this baby was Jesus.
This baby was Jesus.

This Little Child

Words and Music by Scott Wesley Brown

Who would've thought that long ago,
So very far away,
A little Child would be born
And in a manger laid?
And who would've thought this little Child
Was born the King of Kings,
The son of just a carpenter,
But for whom the angels sing?
And who would've thought that as He grew,
And with other children played,
This Child with whom they laughed
　and sang
Would die for them someday?
And who would've thought this little Child
Could make a blind man see,
Feed the hungry, make rich the poor,
And set the sinner free?
Oh, who would've thought this little Child
Was who the prophet said
Would take away the sins of man
And rise up from the dead?

Refrain:
Oh, I believe and I will always sing:
This little Child is the King.
Oh, I believe and I will always sing:
This little Child, He is the King of kings.

Many years have come and gone,
Yet this world remains the same.
Empires have been built and fallen;
Only time has made a change.
Nation against nation,
Brother against brother;
Men so filled with hatred,
Killing one another.
And over half the world is starving
While our banner of decency is torn,
Debating over disarmament,
Killing children before they're born,
And fools who marched to win the right
To justify their sin.
Oh, ev'ry nation that has fallen
Has fallen from within.
Yet in all the midst of this darkness
There is a hope, a light that burns:
This little Child, the King of Kings,
Someday will return.

Refrain

And who would've thought this little Child
Was who the prophet said
Will return to judge this world,
The living and the dead?
Oh, can't you see that long ago,
So very far away,
This little Child, our only hope,
Was born a King that day!

This One's for the Children

Words and Music by Maurice Starr

There are some people living in this world,
They have no food to eat,
They have no place to go.
But we all are God's children,
We have to learn to love one another.
Just remember they could be us,
Remember, we are all brothers.

Refrain:
I'm not trying to darken up your day,
But help others in need
And show them there's a better way.
This one's for the children,
The children of the world.
This one's for the children,
May God keep them in His throne.

Many people are happy
And many people are sad.
Some people have many things
That others can only wish they had.
So, for the sake of the children,
Show them love's the only way to go,
'Cause they're our tomorrow,
And people, they've got to know.

Refrain

This one's for the children,
The children of the world.
This one's for the children,
May God keep them in His throne.
The children of the world.
This one's for the children.

Toyland

Words by Glen MacDonough
Music by Victor Herbert

from the musical *Babes in Toyland*

Toyland! Toyland!
Little girl and boy land,
While you dwell within it,
You are ever happy then.

Childhood's joyland,
Mystic, merry joyland,
Once you pass its borders,
You can never return again.

The Twelve Days of Christmas

Traditional English Carol

On the first day of Christmas,
My true love sent to me
A partridge in a pear tree.

On the second day of Christmas,
My true love sent to me
Two turtle doves
And a partridge in a pear tree.

On the third day of Christmas,
My true love sent to me
Three French hens...
(Etc., counting back to
   "A partridge in a pear tree")

On the fourth day of Christmas,
My true love sent to me
Four calling birds...

On the fifth day of Christmas,
My true love sent to me
Five golden rings...

On the sixth day of Christmas,
My true love gave to me
Six geese a-laying...

On the seventh day of Christmas,
My true love gave to me
Seven swans a-swimming...

On the eighth day of Christmas,
My true love gave to me
Eight maids a-milking...

On the ninth day of Christmas,
My true love gave to me
Nine ladies dancing...

On the tenth day of Christmas,
My true love gave to me
Ten lords a-leaping...

On the eleventh day of Christmas,
My true love gave to me
Eleven pipers piping...

On the twelfth day of Christmas,
My true love gave to me
Twelve drummers drumming...

'Twas the Night Before Christmas

Words by Clement Clark Moore
Music by F. Henri Klickman

'Twas the night before Christmas, when all through the house,
Not a creature was stirring, not even a mouse.
The stockings were hung by the chimney with care,
In the hopes that Saint Nicholas soon would be there.
The children were nestled all snug in their beds,
While visions of sugar plums danced through their heads.
And mamma in her 'kerchief, and I in my cap,
Had just settled our brains for a long winter's nap.

When out on the lawn there arose such a clatter,
I sprang from the bed to see what was the matter.
Away to the window I flew like a flash,
Tore open the shutters and threw up the sash.
The moon on the breast of the new-fallen snow
Gave a lustre of midday to objects below.
When, what to my wondering eyes should appear,
But a miniature sleigh and eight tiny reindeer,

With a little old driver, so lively and quick,
I knew in a moment it must be St. Nick.
More rapid than eagles his coursers they came,
And he whistled, and shouted, and called them by name:
"Now, Dasher! Now, Dancer! Now, Prancer and Vixen!
On, Comet! On Cupid! On, Donner and Blitzen!
To the top of the porch, to the top of the wall!
Now dash away! Dash away! Dash away all!"

As dry leaves that before the wild hurricane fly,
When they meet with an obstacle, mount to the sky,
So up to the house top the coursers they flew,
With the sleigh full of toys, and St. Nicholas too.
And then, in a twinkling, I heard on the roof
The prancing and pawing of each little hoof.
As I drew in my hand, and was turning around,
Down the chimney St. Nicholas came with a bound.

He was dressed all in fur, from his head to his foot,
And his clothes were all tarnished with ashes and soot;
A bundle of toys he had flung on his back,
And he looked like a peddler just opening his pack.
His eyes, how they twinkled! His dimples, how merry!
His cheeks were like roses, his nose like a cherry!
His droll little mouth was drawn up like a bow,
And the beard of his chin was as white as the snow.

The stump of a pipe he held tight in his teeth,
And the smoke, it encircled his head like a wreath.
He had a broad face and a little round belly
That shook, when he laughed, like a bowl full of jelly.
He was chubby and plump, a right jolly old elf,
And I laughed when I saw him, in spite of myself;
A wink of his eye, and a twist of his head,
Soon gave me to know I had nothing to dread.

He spoke not a word, but went straight to his work,
And filled all the stockings; then turned with a jerk,
And laying his finger aside of his nose,
And giving a nod, up the chimney he rose.
He sprang to his sleigh, to his team gave a whistle,
And away they all fled like the down of a thistle.
But I heard him exclaim, ere he drove out of sight,
"Happy Christmas to all, and to all a good night!"

Unto Us (Isaiah 9)

Words and Music by Larry Bryant and Lesa Bryant

People who walk in the darkness
Are going to behold a great light;
Those in the land of the shadow
Will all say goodbye to the night.
And joy will fill the kingdom
For He will bring you freedom,
The chains of fallen Eden
Will be shattered by His might.

Refrain:
Unto us a child is born
And He will sit on David's throne.
And the Government will be
On the shoulders of this King.
He will reign forevermore.
Unto us a child is born.

Ev'ry boot that has marched to the battle
Will finally be set aflame;
Fear of the enemy's torment
Will rise up in smoke just the same.
For He comes to bring you peace,
His kingdom will increase,
He's coming to release
Ev'ry man from sin and shame.

Refrain

And His name will be Wonderful Counselor,
Mighty God, Prince of Peace.

Refrain

Unto us a child is born.
Unto us a child is born!

Up on the Housetop

Words and Music by B.R. Handy

Up on the housetop reindeer pause,
Out jumps good old Santa Claus;
Down through the chimney with lots of toys,
All for the little ones, Christmas joys.

Refrain:
Ho, ho, ho! Who wouldn't go?
Ho, ho, ho! Who wouldn't go?
Up on the housetop, click, click, click,
Down through the chimney with good Saint Nick.

First comes the stocking of little Nell;
Oh, dear Santa, fill it well.
Give her a dolly that laughs and cries,
One that will open and shut her eyes.

Refrain

Look in the stocking of little Will,
Oh, just see what a glorious fill!
Here is a hammer and lots of tacks,
Whistle and ball and a whip that cracks.

Refrain

Wassail, Wassail

Old English Air

Wassail, wassail, all over the town!
Our bread it is white and our ale it is brown;
Our bowl is made of the maple tree;
So here, my good fellow, I'll drink to thee.

The wass'ling bowl with a toast within,
Come, fill it up now unto the brim.
Come, fill it up that we may all see,
With the wassailing bowl, I'll drink to thee.

Come, butler, bring us a bowl of your best,
And we hope your soul in heaven shall rest.
But if you bring us a bowl too small,
Then down shall go butler and bowl and all.

Watchman, Tell Us of the Night

Traditional

Watchman, tell us of the night,
What its signs of promise are.
Trav'ler, o'er yon mountain's height,
See that glory beaming star.
Watchman, does its beauteous ray
Aught of joy or hope foretell?
Trav'ler, yes, it brings the day,
Promised day of Israel.

Watchman, tell us of the night,
Higher yet that star ascends.
Trav'ler, blessedness and light,
Peace and truth, its course portends.
Watchman, will its beams alone
Gild the spot that gave them birth!
Trav'ler, ages are its own;
See it bursts o'er all the earth.

Watchman, tell us of the night,
For the morning seems to dawn.
Trav'ler, darkness takes its flight,
Doubt and terror are withdrawn.
Watchman, let thy wand'rings cease,
Hie thee to thy quiet home.
Trav'ler, lo, the Prince of Peace,
Lo, the Son of God is come.

We Are Santa's Elves

Music and Lyrics by Johnny Marks

Ho ho ho!
Ho ho ho!
We are Santa's elves.

We are Santa's elves,
Filling Santa's shelves
With a toy for each girl and boy.
Oh, we are Santa's elves.

We work hard all day,
But our work is play.
Dolls we try out,
See if they cry out.
We are Santa's elves.

We've a special job each year.
We don't like to brag.
Christmas Eve we always fill Santa's bag.

Santa knows who's good,
Do the things you should.
And we bet you
He won't forget you.
We are Santa's elves.

Ho ho ho!
Ho ho ho!
We are Santa's elves.
Ho ho!

We Need a Little Christmas

Music and Lyric by Jerry Herman

from the musical *Mame*

Haul out the holly,
Put up the tree before my
Spirit falls again.
Fill up the stocking,
I may be rushing things, but
Deck the halls again now.

For we need a little Christmas,
Right this very minute,
Candles in the window,
Carols at the spinet.
Yes, we need a little Christmas,
Right this very minute,
It hasn't snowed a single flurry,
But Santa, dear, we're in a hurry.

So climb down the chimney,
Turn on the brightest string of
Lights I've ever seen,
Slice up the fruitcake,
It's time we hung some tinsel
On that evergreen bough.

For I've grown a little leaner,
Grown a little colder,
Grown a little sadder,
Grown a little older.
And I need a little angel,
Sitting on my shoulder,
Need a little Christmas now!

For we need a little music,
Need a little laughter,
Need a little singing,
Ringing through the rafter.
And we need a little snappy
"Happy ever after,"
Need a little Christmas now!

We Three Kings of Orient Are

Words and Music by John H. Hopkins, Jr.

We three kings of Orient are;
Bearing gifts we traverse afar,
Field and fountain, moor and mountain,
Following yonder star.

Refrain:
O star of wonder, star of night,
Star with royal beauty bright,
Westward leading, still proceeding,
Guide us to thy perfect light.

Born a King on Bethlehem's plain,
Gold I bring to crown Him again,
King forever, ceasing never
Over us all to reign.

Refrain

Frankincense to offer have I;
Incense owns a Deity nigh;
Prayer and praising, all men raising,
Worship Him, God most high.

Refrain

Myrrh is mine; its bitter perfume
Breathes a life of gathering gloom;
Sorr'wing, sighing, bleeding, dying,
Sealed in the stone-cold tomb.

Refrain

Glorious now, behold Him arise,
King and God and sacrifice,
Alleluia, alleluia,
Earth to heav'n replies.

Refrain

Wexford Carol

Traditional Irish Carol

Good people all, this Christmas time,
Consider well and bear in mind,
What our good God for us has done
In sending His beloved Son.
With Mary holy we should pray
To God with love this Christmas day;
In Bethlehem upon that morn
There was a blessed Messiah born.

The night before that happy tide
The noble Virgin and her guide
Were long time seeking up and down
To find a lodging in the town.
But mark how all things came to pass:
From ev'ry door repelled, alas!
As long foretold, their refuge all
Was but a humble ox's stall.

Near Bethlehem did shepherds keep
Their flocks of lambs and feeding sheep;
To whom God's angels did appear,
Which put the shepherds in great fear.
"Prepare and go," the angels said,
"To Bethlehem, be not afraid;
For there you'll find, this happy morn,
A princely babe, sweet Jesus born."

With thankful heart and joyful mind,
The shepherds went the Babe to find,
And as God's angel had foretold,
They did our Savior Christ behold.
Within a manger He was laid,
And by his side the Virgin maid,
Attending on the Lord of life,
Who came on earth to end all strife.

There were three wise men from afar
Directed by a glorious star,
And on they wandered night and day
Until they came where Jesus lay,
And when they came unto that place
Where our beloved Messiah was,
They humbly cast them at His feet,
With gifts of gold and incense sweet.

What Are You Doing New Year's Eve?

By Frank Loesser

Maybe it's much too early in the game,
Ah, but I thought I'd ask you just the same,
What are you doing New Year's, New Year's Eve?
Wonder whose arms will hold you good and tight,
When it's exactly twelve o'clock that night,
Welcoming in the new year, New Year's Eve?

Maybe I'm crazy to suppose
I'd ever be the one you chose
Out of a thousand invitations you'll receive.
Ah, but in case I stand one little chance,
Here comes the jackpot question in advance:
What are you doing New Year's, New Year's Eve?

What Child Is This?

Words by William C. Dix
16th Century English Melody

What Child is this, who, laid to rest,
On Mary's lap is sleeping?
Whom angels greet with anthems sweet,
While shepherds watch are keeping?

Refrain:
This, this is Christ the King,
Whom shepherds guard and angels sing:
Haste, haste to bring Him laud,
The Babe, the Son of Mary.

Why lies He in such mean estate
Where ox and ass are feeding?
Good Christian, fear, for sinners here
The silent Word is pleading.

Refrain

So bring Him incense, gold, and myrrh,
Come peasant, king to own Him;
The King of kings salvation brings,
Let loving hearts enthrone Him.

Refrain

What Made the Baby Cry?

Words and Music by William J. Golay

On a cold night, late December,
As the snow fell to earth,
That's the one night we remember
When a woman gave birth.
And for miles and miles around,
A baby's cry was the only sound.

Did He know the world was
　filled with pain?
Could He feel all the hunger
　and the shame?
Or did He know about the way
　He would die
And the reason why?
Is that what made the baby cry?
Is that what made the baby cry?

As His Mother turned to hold Him,
Her face filled with joy.
He grew quiet as She told Him
He was more than just her baby boy.
And for miles and miles around,
Her lullaby was the only sound.

Did she know the world was
　filled with pain?
Could she feel all the hunger
　and the shame?
Or did she know about the way
　He would die
And the reason why?
Is that what made her baby cry?
Is that what made her baby cry?

And as He fell asleep,
She wiped away His tears.
But the question still remains:
Have we changed in two thousand years?

Don't you know the world is
　still in pain?
Can't you see all the hunger
　and the shame?
Did we forget about the way
　that He died
And the reason why?
Would we still make the baby cry?
Would we still make the baby cry?

When Christ Was Born of Mary Free

Traditional English Carol

When Christ was born of Mary free,
In Bethlehem that fair city,
Angels sung there with mirth and glee:
"In excelsis gloria."

Refrain:
In excelsis gloria,
In excelsis gloria,
In excelsis gloria.

This King is come to save mankind,
As in the scripture truths we find,
Therefore this song we have in mind:
"In excelsis gloria."

Refrain

Then, dearest Lord, for Thy great grace,
Grant us in bliss to see Thy face,
That we may sing to Thy solace:
"In excelsis gloria."

Refrain

When Love Came Down

Written by Chris Eaton

Close your eyes and share the dream;
Let ev'ryone on earth believe.
The Child was born, the stars shone bright,
And Love came down at Christmas time,
And Love came down at Christmas time.

Christmas Eve, two A.M.;
Heavy snow is falling down.
And the streets, clothed in white,
Echo songs that were sung by candlelight.

We're alive, we can breathe;
But do we really care for this world in need?
There's a choice we must make each and every day.

Refrain:
So close your eyes and share the dream;
Let ev'ryone on earth believe.
The Child was born, the stars shone bright,
And Love came down at Christmas time,
And Love came down at Christmas time.

So merry Christmas ev'ryone,
And peace throughout the year.
The time has come to celebrate,
So let your voices fill the air.
Ev'ryone, watch and pray
That the sun will shine on a brighter day.
Join your hands, lift them high
For this gift of life.
When Love came down at Christmas time.
When Love came down at Christmas time.
When Love came down at Christmas time.
When Love came down at Christmas time.

Refrain Twice

When Santa Claus Gets Your Letter

Music and Lyrics by Johnny Marks

Christmas comes but once a year,
With presents 'round the tree.
When you write to Santa Claus,
Take this tip from me.

When Santa Claus gets your letter,
You know what he will say:
"Have you been good the way you should
On ev'ry single day?"

When Santa gets your letter
To ask for Christmas toys,
He'll take a look in his good book
He keeps for girls and boys.

He'll stroke his beard, his eyes will glow,
And at your name he'll peer;
It takes a little time, you know,
To check back one whole year!

When Santa Claus gets your letter,
I really do believe,
You'll head his list, you won't be missed,
By Santa on Christmas Eve.

Where Are You Christmas?

Words and Music by Will Jennings, James Horner and Mariah Carey

from the film *Dr. Seuss' How the Grinch Stole Christmas*

Where are you, Christmas?
Why can't I find you?
Why have you gone away?
Where is the laughter
You used to bring me?
Why can't I hear music play?
My world is changing.
I'm rearranging.
Does that mean Christmas changes too?

Where are you, Christmas?
Do you remember
The one you used to know?
I'm not the same one.
See what the time's done.
Is that why you have let me go?

Oh, Christmas is here, ev'rywhere.
Oh, Christmas is here, if you care.
If there is love in your heart and your mind,
You will feel like Christmas all the time.

I feel you, Christmas,
I know I found you.
You never fade away.
Oh, the joy of Christmas
Stays here inside us,
Fills each and ev'ry heart with love.

Where are you, Christmas?
Fill your heart with love.

While Shepherds Watched Their Flocks by Night

Words by Nahum Tate
Music by George Frideric Handel

While shepherds watched their flocks by night,
All seated on the ground,
The angel of the Lord came down,
And glory shone around.

"Fear not," said he, for mighty dread
Had seized their troubled mind.
"Glad tidings of great joy I bring
To you and all mankind.

"To you in David's town this day
Is born of David's line
A Savior, who is Christ the Lord,
And this shall be the sign.

"The heav'nly babe you there shall find
To human view displayed,
All meanly wrapped in swathing bands
And in a manger laid."

Thus spoke the seraph, and forthwith
Appeared a shining throng
Of angels praising God on high,
Who thus addressed their song:

"All glory be to God on high,
And on the earth be peace;
Goodwill henceforth from heav'n to earth
Begin and never cease!"

The White World of Winter

Words by Mitchell Parish
Music by Hoagy Carmichael

In this wonderful white world of winter,
Darling, we'll have a wonderful time;
First, we'll ride side by side through the hinter
And rondelay to the sleighbell's merrie chime;
Then we'll ski fancy free down the mountains
And take those chances all silly people do.
If there's ever a moment you are freezin',
Just a little squeezin' could be mighty pleasin',
In this wonderful white world of winter,
I'm fallin' head over heels over you.

In this wonderful white world of winter,
Darling, we'll have a wonderful time;
If we prayed it would snow all this winter,
I ask ya, is that a terr'ble horr'ble crime?
I can't wait till we skate on Lake Happy
And sup a hot buttered cup in the afterglow.
If there's ever a moment you're not laughin',
Maybe a toboggan split your little noggin'.
In this wonderful white world of winter,
I'm thinkin' you are the sweetest one I know.

Who Would Imagine a King

Words and Music by Mervyn Warren and Hallerin Hilton Hill

from the Touchstone Motion Picture *The Preacher's Wife*

Mommies and daddies always believe
That their little angels are special indeed.
And you could grow up to be anything.
But who would imagine a King?

A shepherd or teacher is what you could be,
Or maybe a fisherman out on the sea,
Or maybe a carpenter building things.
But who would imagine a King?

It was so clear when the wise men arrived
And the angels were singing your name
That the world would be diff'rent 'cause you were alive.
That's why heaven stood still to proclaim.

One day an angel said quietly
That soon he would bring something special to me.
And of all of the wonderful gifts he could bring,
Who would imagine,
Who could imagine,
Who would imagine a King?

Winds Through the Olive Trees

19th Century American Carol

Winds through the olive trees,
Softly did blow,
'Round little Bethlehem,
Long, long ago.

Sheep on the hillside lay,
White as the snow,
Shepherds were watching them,
Long, long ago.

Then from the starry skies,
Angels bent low,
Singing their songs of joy,
Long, long ago.

For in a manger bed,
Cradled, we know,
Christ came to Bethlehem,
Long, long ago.

Wonderful Christmastime

Words and Music by McCartney

The mood is right, the spirit's up,
We're here tonight and that's enough.
Simply having a wonderful Christmastime.
Simply having a wonderful Christmastime.

The party's on, the feeling's here
That only comes this time of year.
Simply having a wonderful Christmastime.
Simply having a wonderful Christmastime.

The choir of children sing their song.
Ding dong, ding dong.
Ding, dong, ding.
Ooh, ooh.
Do do do do do do do.

We're simply having a wonderful Christmastime.
Simply having a wonderful Christmastime.

The word is out about the town,
To lift a glass, oh, don't look down.
Simply having a wonderful Christmastime.
Simply having a wonderful Christmastime.

The choir of children sing their song.
(They practiced all year long.)
Ding dong, ding dong, ding dong,
Ding dong, ding dong, ding dong,
Dong, dong, dong, dong.

The party's on, the spirit's up.
We're here tonight and that's enough.
Simply having a wonderful Christmastime.
We're simply having a wonderful Christmastime.

You Make It Feel Like Christmas

Words and Music by Neil Diamond

Look at us now, part of it all.
In spite of it all, we're still around.
Lovers in love, just like we were.
Being apart's a lonely sound.
When people ask how we stay together,
I say you never let me down.

And you make it feel like Christmas
Even when things go wrong.
I hear the sound of Christmas in your song
All year long.

Look at the sun shining on me.
Nowhere could be a better place.
Lovers in love, that's what we are.
I reach for that star out there in space.

'Cause you make it feel like Christmas
Even when things go wrong.
I hear the sound of Christmas in your song
All year long.

Sleepy we are, but happy together.
Sounds of forever greet the day.
So wake up the kids, put on some tea.
Light up the tree; it's Christmas day.

Yeah, you make it feel like Christmas
Even when things go wrong.
I hear the sound of Christmas in your song
All year long.
All year long.
Light up the tree; it's Christmas time.

Index by First Line

More Collections from the Lyric Library

The Lyric Library lets you bring more completeness and accuracy to your song repertoire. Rediscover a nearly forgotten gem, wallow in nostalgia, or browse through examples of great songwriting and enjoy the words as poetry set to music. Each jam-packed collection features complete lyrics to over 200 songs.

BROADWAY VOLUME I
00240201 $14.95

BROADWAY VOLUME II
00240205 $14.95

CHRISTMAS
00240206 $14.95

CLASSIC ROCK
00240183 $14.95

CONTEMPORARY CHRISTIAN
00240184 $14.95

COUNTRY
00240204 $14.95

EARLY ROCK 'N' ROLL
00240203 $14.95

LOVE SONGS
00240186 $14.95

POP/ROCK BALLADS
00240187 $14.95

See our website for a complete contents list for each volume:
www.halleonard.com

FOR MORE INFORMATION, SEE YOUR LOCAL MUSIC DEALER,
OR WRITE TO:

HAL•LEONARD®
CORPORATION
7777 W. BLUEMOUND RD. P.O. BOX 13819 MILWAUKEE, WI 53213

Prices, contents and availability subject to change without notice.